THE
LIFE
BRIEF

THE
LIFE
BRIEF

A Playbook For No-Regrets Living

BONNIE WAN

SIMON ELEMENT

New York London Toronto Sydney New Delhi

SIMON ELEMENT

An Imprint of Simon & Schuster, Inc.
1230 Avenue of the Americas
New York, NY 10020

Some names and identifying characteristics have been changed. Some dialogue has been re-created.

First Simon Element hardcover edition January 2024

SIMON ELEMENT is a trademark of Simon & Schuster, Inc.

Simon & Schuster: Celebrating 100 Years of Publishing in 2024

For information about special discounts for bulk purchases, please contact Simon & Schuster Special Sales at 1-866-506-1949 or business@simonandschuster.com.

The Simon & Schuster Speakers Bureau can bring authors to your live event. For more information or to book an event, contact the Simon & Schuster Speakers Bureau at 1-866-248-3049 or visit our website at www.simonspeakers.com.

Interior design by Laura Levatino

Manufactured in the United States of America

10 9 8 7 6 5 4 3 2 1

Library of Congress Cataloging-in-Publication Data has been applied for.

ISBN 978-1-9821-9550-2
ISBN 978-1-9821-9551-9 (ebook)

TO CHIP, MY BELOVED ONE.
Thank you for letting me tell our story, bumps and all.
I love you madly.

ZIG, ILA, RUBY, AND MABEL.
This book was written with you in my heart.
May you find your voice, live your truth, and carve a path
of your own making.

CONTENTS

CONTENTS

PART 2:
Get Clear

PART 3:
Get Active

THE
LIFE
BRIEF

GET READY

LET'S BE BRIEF

What do you want?

It's a simple question, right? We ask it all the time, when deciding what to eat, how to spend our day, or what we'd like for our birthday. But that's not what I'm asking.

I'm not asking, what are you in the mood for, or what do you *think* you want? And I'm definitely not asking, what do your parents, your partner, or your friends want for you.

What I'm asking is this: In your heart of hearts, *what do you really, really want?* What do you want in your life that you haven't even admitted to yourself?

This is the driving question of the Life Brief.

INTRODUCTION

THE CHAOS BEFORE THE CLARITY

It was April 2010, and my life looked picture-perfect.

I was married to a handsome, emotionally present man. We lived in a one-of-a-kind house at the edges of wine country in Northern California. I had just returned to work after giving birth to our third child to run one of our agency's biggest accounts.

On the outside, things looked damn good. But inside, I was drowning and depleted and full of questions. *Am I with the right person? Is Chip the right partner for me? Can I keep up with and hold on to this life we've created?*

And perhaps most unbearable, *What happens if my answers are no?*

To be honest, these questions terrified me. What answers would I uncover on the other side? The sheer act of asking felt like an admission of weakness or failure, prompting punishing self-talk. *What's wrong with me? Why can't I see how good I have it? Why can't I suck it up and get on with it?*

After all, I'd never doubted my husband's goodness. I was instantly attracted to him from the moment I spotted him on the other side of a packed conference room. At the time we were working at the same agency on a big car account—hardly a romantic setting—and yet when I looked over, his vitality instantly captivated me.

Who is that? I wondered.

The answer, I would discover, was Chip, someone who is inquisitive, openhearted, and lit up from within.

But you know the way time and everyday stresses can dull your senses? That's what was happening with us. We were juggling careers and childcare for three kids under the age of five. Chip was launching a documentary film business while my job as an advertising strategist

xii

demanded long hours, travel, and a two-plus-hour round-trip daily commute even when I wasn't meeting clients on the other side of the country.

When we weren't "dividing and conquering," we were negotiating, deliberating, or downright arguing. Crushed by the weight of work, caregiving, and housekeeping, I grew increasingly critical and borderline resentful. We were wrecked from sleeplessness and wracked with financial anxiety. It felt as if we were constantly on the verge of spinning out of control.

As our lives grew more chaotic, so did the distance between us. Yes, the business trips pulled us apart. But the distance took place at home, too. We would be right there in the same room, caught up in our own worlds—different headspaces and emotional states. I might be lost in a barrage of work emails or navigating a tricky client request, while nursing or rocking the baby. Meanwhile, he'd be a few feet away, absorbed in his next production or watching a football game while entertaining two toddlers.

"Babe, what should we have for dinner?" he'd ask, innocently enough.

Dinner? Our biggest client just put our account into review.

The urgency and intensity of my stress ratcheted up with every text or email. Irritated, I'd snap, "I can't think about dinner right now."

And with that, we dropped back in our bubbles.

At the highest levels, our interests and values aligned—social creatures fueled and fed by our connection to family, friends, and community. But our styles clashed—across everything from how we viewed money to how we parented and made decisions. I was impatient, demanding, and a perfectionist. He moved slower, taking his time to navigate the madness, overwhelmed by my standards, not to mention his own. This hadn't mattered much when it was just the two of us—when the pace was slow and stakes were low. But now, with three young kids and intense work pressure, every small thing felt big.

I spent countless nights weighing the pros and cons of our relationship.

One rainy day after a particularly heated argument, I sat in the grocery store parking lot, unable to get out of the car. I listened to the rain as it hammered against metal and glass. I phoned a dear friend and laid my frustrations bare, giving voice to questions I had not previously dared to ask aloud.

What if we're just too different?

What if I don't have what it takes?

Are marriage, parenting, and life supposed to be this hard?

Does staying in this marriage mean losing myself?

Once admitted and voiced, these questions became vividly real and impossible to ignore. But the answers did not appear that day in the grocery store parking lot.

WEEKS PASSED AND THE UNCERTAINTY CONTINUED TO SWIRL in my mind. There was a time when I might have brought my worries to Chip, but my gnawing questions felt too raw, too dangerous—I feared that if I said them aloud, I would set in motion the beginning of the end.

Not long after that parking lot call, I took a business trip that brought me back to my hometown. After a long day of meetings, I was physically exhausted, but my brain was still churning away. Instead of staying at a hotel with my team, I decided to spend the night with my parents. Part of me hoped that the familiarity of family and my mom's cooking could calm my emotional turbulence.

But there was something about being back in my childhood home that intensified my angst. I might be a mom of three and a strategy director at a major ad agency, but inside I felt like the kid I'd been twenty years before: someone who'd learned to override inner unrest and stuff it behind a bright smile and confident, can-do spirit.

Shutting the door to my old bedroom, I breathed in the remnants of my childhood. The rainbow bedspread, mixtapes, and *Interview* magazine covers were long gone, but the glossy white furniture set was arranged just as it had been in 1988. There on the floor against my bed, I let my tears flow, face buried into a pillow, hoping my parents wouldn't wake and wonder what the hell was going on.

Not that *I* had a grasp on what the hell was going on. My teenage self would have been wowed by the life I had created. I was the vision of success she had imagined and dreamed of, down to the hot-pink suede Miu Miu pumps I kicked off across the room.

So why the hell was I so miserable?

What was *wrong* with me?

Something had to give, but what?

There were those questions again, looping back and around, no closer to a decision or solution. They were quiet yet insistent:

I can't do this anymore.

I really can't.

Then, something unexpected happened. As soon as I allowed my despair to hit bottom, the moment I committed to change yet admitted to not knowing how, I was hit with a sense of strange familiarity.

Wait.

I *recognized* this confusion.

I had met a similar feeling, hundreds of times before, with my clients and their brands. For much of my professional life, I had sat across from people asking themselves questions about purpose, values, and vision. For years, I had cultivated a list of questions that I could use to help clients get to the heart of their truths and use that clarity to unlock real and lasting change.

Was it possible that I could turn those questions on myself to achieve the same outcome?

After decades as a strategist, I knew how to uncover the essence of what matters to others and translate that into clear and actionable strategies. But I had lost sight of it for myself. I was so caught up in the busyness of each day—back-to-back client meetings, pumping milk in dirty airport bathrooms, long commutes to and from the office, often not returning until my husband and kids were fast asleep. My own sense of what mattered and why I was working so hard had all but evaporated from my consciousness.

I had been circling in confusion for months. And it wasn't until that night that I began to turn this curiosity and precision on my own life, cutting to the heart of what I wanted most. For the first time in a very long time, I felt a glimmer of hope that I might be able to make meaning out of my own emotional mess. But first, I realized, I had to do what I advise my clients.

To get to the essence of what I really wanted, I would need to cut through the clutter of my confusion. To make it manifest, I'd have to clearly and boldly declare what I wanted so that I could act on it. And for it to be meaningful and genuinely motivating, I had to make it sticky and brief.

Pulling myself off the floor, I rummaged through my old desk, found a half-used Mead spiral notebook. I started scribbling, mad and messy. Away from Chip, our kids, and work, I was forced to acknowledge the things that weren't working. I was willing to leave everything on the page if it helped me find my way home.

Lost, desperate, with my sleeves wet from snot and tears, I was on the way to writing my first Life Brief.

HOW TO USE THIS BOOK

I make meaning out of messiness. It's my job and my passion. As partner and head of brand strategy at the storied advertising agency Goodby Silverstein & Partners (GS&P), my job is to help companies understand why they exist so they can find the simplest path through chaos, complexity, and confusion.

With the Life Brief, I now do the same for everyday people. A moment to state the obvious here. You are not a brand. You're much more complex than a car, an app, or a bag of chips. But we *all* need a way to cut through the noise—and that's what brand strategy is designed to do. The Life Brief distills the practice of brand strategy into its simplest, clearest, and most effective form to help people get clear about their careers, their families, their creative outlets, as well as their relationships to themselves, their communities, and the world.

I created the Life Brief as a tool to cut through the mess and muck in my own life—the critical voices, the limiting beliefs, the self-doubt, and, at times, the paralyzing fear. Only then was I able to surface and see my own values and vision for my life. The Life Brief transformed my life in ways that are profound, exhilarating, and empowering. And since I've begun sharing it with others, I know I'm not alone.

What Is a Life Brief?

The most important tool used by every strategist and creative agency is what's known as a "creative brief." This single-page, single-minded document concisely yet vividly captures a company's essence and ambition. Great briefs distill complex problems into sharp and sticky strategies that focus our attention, unlock solutions, and inspire action.

When drafting creative briefs, strategists use questions to guide, if not *force*, clarity about the essential building blocks of a brand. The flow of these questions on a single page pushes you to connect the dots and culminates in a single-minded strategic idea for a company's future direction.

The Life Brief is, at its simplest, a creative brief for your life.

But because you're not a brand, the Life Brief doesn't follow the same format as the creative briefs we write for brands. What we're aiming for here are five clear, bold, declarative statements about what you want in the areas of your life that matter most, summed up in a sharp and sticky phrase that you can use to guide your decisions and drive your actions.

This sounds simple, but it's a transformative process. In order to get to statements that are focused, specific, and above all, penetratingly honest, we first need to go wide—with warm-ups, exercises, reflective prompts, and questions designed to unlock your curiosity, creativity, and clarity.

Ultimately, the Life Brief is a practice of alignment between who you are, what you believe, and how you live—one that begins with that crucial question:

What do you really, really want?

That was the question I asked myself that weepy night in my childhood bedroom.

And it was the one I posed to the standing-room-only audience in my very first workshop for the Life Brief. My agency had invited senior leaders to teach something personal to our colleagues as part of our employee wellness program.

When it came to my turn, I was initially stumped. Our agency president led Run Club, our managing partner taught yoga, and others shared their passions and crafts. I couldn't think of any hobbies or interests I felt inspired to teach. But then, I was hit by an idea. What if I shared the way I had saved my marriage, harmonized work and family, and reconnected with my sense of joy, by writing a creative brief for my life?

My nerves intensified as the class approached. Teaching this practice would require me to share some very private and dark moments in my personal life. One of the limiting beliefs we've collectively harbored as a society is that leaders, especially women, should present an impeccable front at all times. Wear your game face, be the badass, and strut your swagger. These were the mantras of the moment. And here I was, about to get vulnerable: throwing open the closet doors of my life and allowing my personal mess to spill out. Would I lose the respect of my colleagues? Would I lose face? Would I ruin my career?

The session was open to all employees at the agency. I couldn't tell what terrified me more: getting personal with people I didn't know or exposing myself to those I worked alongside every day. I paced the hall as I awaited my turn to speak. I meandered in and out of the restroom. I considered calling everything off and blaming it on a mysterious illness. But because I was already relishing what my very first Life Brief had made possible—a more fulfilling marriage, a beautiful, creative, and colorful life in Portland, Oregon—I knew it was something I wanted to share with others.

Once I got in the room, I was shocked by the mix of attendees—creative teams, the head of production, junior employees, and interns. My boss was there, next to our head of HR. My fellow strategists were there, along with people I mentored and people I had never met. I took a deep breath and said to myself, *Here we go*, diving into my story as the room hushed.

I unpacked the Life Brief practice to the crowded room. I disclosed the marriage troubles that started it all. I openly admitted that I struggled with juggling my career and family. I explained the steps I had taken in creating the brief, the kinds of questions I asked that pushed me to answer them with naked honesty, and the way this process had led to personal and creative breakthroughs. I shared how I had used the tools of our trade to examine my personal challenges in a new light, and in doing so, I had uncovered a practice and path to clarity that might work for others.

So. What do *you* want?

I asked the question as a palpable tension gripped the room. There was quiet rustling as folks sat up straight in their seats. Then the room went dead silent—I could see that people were thinking deeply about their own lives and asking their own gripping questions.

If you cringe at the question or find it off-putting, that's okay.

I've been there myself, resisting anything that smells of or signals self-help.

But here's what I've learned. If we never allow ourselves to ask and honestly answer this simple question, we run the risk of never getting what we want. If we don't check in with ourselves about our own dreams and desires, we might end up following someone else's plans, feeling confused about our own, or lost as to why we're feeling unfulfilled.

Applying this practice to my life has deepened and saved my marriage (not once, but twice), centered my parenting, and propelled my career far beyond what I could have imagined. It's helped me turn those nagging questions that once felt agonizing and unthinkable into springboards for action.

It's why I've come to think of the Life Brief as the shortest path between where you are now and what you really, really want.

There are many wonderful healing tools, practices, and programs out there—I've certainly benefitted from some of them—but what sets the Life Brief apart is that it's specifically designed to cut through the clutter and get right to the heart of what matters most.

So, here's my invitation to you. Suspend your doubts and disbelief. Jump in and give this practice a go. Ask the question. Let it sink in and stir. Your answer might end up surprising you.

Start Practicing, Stop Planning

The Life Brief is a practice for getting clear on what you want, not a plan for how to get there. Don't get me wrong: I'm a fan of plans when it comes to finances, ad campaigns, and organizing events. But when it comes to navigating life, plans prevent us from seeing the possibilities around us. When we're so attached to one path or one outcome, we lose our peripheral vision and fail to see the unexpected invitations emerging around us, beckoning for our attention.

As the poet David Whyte once said, "What you can plan is too small for you to live." Plans are usually based on facts we already know or can see from where we're standing, opinions we already hold. But life is peppered with surprise and serendipity that are impossible to plan for or around.

Plans are about seeing every step, executing each action as we see it from right here, right now. They dictate, often in great detail, the "how." It's that dictating that we want to move away from. That's why in advertising, we use creative briefs to capture a clear ambition, idea, or desired outcome, but we leave open *how* we get there.

I get the appeal of plans. They give us the *feeling* that we're in control—that we can control life itself. Yet, the expansiveness of life lies in that which we cannot plan or predict. Instead of a plan, I think of the Life Brief as a practice—a practice of exploration, for seeking, examining, and acting on your innermost truth. It's a process of getting clear about what you really want in life and opening yourself to receiving it as it comes. It is a method you can revisit every time you need to reconnect with your own sense of purpose and agency.

The Life Brief practice is also not something you have to leap into overnight—it's not about making drastic life changes or holding yourself to restrictive resolutions.

Instead, the series of writing and thinking exercises in this book will help you tune in to your inner voice—the one that you push aside in favor of what's "practical" or what's right in front of you—so you can hear the essence of your calling. You'll distill your desires into a short list of what you're ready for right now. You'll be able to wrap it in a specific phrase that brings your entire Life Brief into focus anytime you need to remember what really matters.

And you'll learn how to create different Life Briefs for different parts of your life—starting with the four areas where people spend most of their time: relationships, work, community, and self. Your "Big Four" don't need to fit into traditional cookie-cutter boxes. A relationship can mean anything from romantic relationships to relationships with your colleagues, children, parents, or even pets. Your work can be your livelihood, side hustle, education, or other areas where you want to grow. Your community consists of the safety net of trust and understanding that you're a part of, whether that be a circle of friends, your place of worship, or a cause to which you're committed. And "self" can contain everything about how you feel, see, and treat yourself in relation to the world around you.

In his book *The Three Marriages*, poet David Whyte refers to our relationships with others, work, and self as "marriages." He warns us that we cannot choose between them. Each of these marriages is nonnegotiable—meaning that if you allow one to fall, the others will eventually follow. Yet, it's easy to sacrifice one aspect of our lives seemingly in service of the others. For many of us, our relationship with ourself is the hardest to prioritize or fight for—few of us are encouraged to care for ourselves, nourish ourselves, stoke our own fires. The Life Brief will guide you to connect to what matters most within each of your vital relationships, especially the one with yourself.

What matters most to you can and will shift over time. The Life Brief isn't a one-and-done list. You can create one whenever you need to break through the noise around you and re-establish clarity in your life. I do one every time I feel stuck, lost, or confused in any given part of my life. At pivotal moments, I have created a Life Brief for every area of my life.

This book will help you do the same. The more you practice and allow your Life Briefs to guide you, the faster you'll start to recognize when you've lost your way and need to hit the page and create a new Life Brief. And as with any practice, the more you use it, the easier and more automatic it will become.

This book is meant to create a safe place for experimentation. It's an invitation to free your inhibitions and open up in low-stakes yet new ways. This process is designed to help you take leaps in the privacy of your own existence—try on ideas, test out truths, say them aloud, get into relationship with them, notice how you feel, and get comfortable with things that used to be uncomfortable.

It's a strategy that transforms vulnerability into action.

Get Messy, Get Clear, Get Active

The Life Brief has three distinct parts: Get Messy, Get Clear, and Get Active. The first phase, Get Messy, will guide you through the disarray and confusion clogging your mind, blocking you from realizing what's underneath: your sacred soul desires. It gives you the space to explore what you really, really want with honesty so that you can be present with what arises. Getting Messy will help you identify the brilliant and deeply personal "threads" of your life—your unique collection of values, beliefs, and desires—and shake them all out onto the table, using questions and creative exercises to stoke, stimulate, and cajole them into expression.

Once you've given yourself permission to Get Messy, the next step is to sort and separate what matters from what doesn't. Getting Clear is about working with the vibrant yet chaotic pile of threads you've collected when Getting Messy—to understand the role each plays in your life so that you can weave them together into a beautiful tapestry. This stage is a process of distilling, sharpening, and zeroing in on the essence of what you want—then pushing it to its boldest place.

Finally, Getting Active is where we walk the walk of our Briefs, harnessing our personal agency and understanding that it is we who are the creators of our lives, not our circumstances. This is where the dance between you and the world takes place. You'll see how your actions invite new reactions and interactions from people around you. This is a dance where tiny movements generate huge effects, where surprising outcomes are revealed in serendipitous ways. You'll practice staying committed to your Life Brief, working through fears as they arise. You'll be tested, taken to the edges of doubt and disillusionment before each breakthrough. So many times, I've come to the cliff of giving up or giving in, when surrendering to *what is* unlocks the magic of *what will be.*

During each phase, I will share questions, prompts, and exercises to help you break through the clutter, identify the fears and beliefs holding you back, and create a Life Brief—and a life—that is wholly your own.

I'm also going to share my story, along with the stories of others who used this practice to declare what they so desperately desired. But make no mistake: this book is about you. These stories are here to walk you through the practice of moving from mess to clarity to action, but while everyone's life circumstances are unique, the journey is universal.

The Life Brief is designed to light you up and awaken parts of yourself that have been dormant. It asks you to use muscles you may not have used in a while. So, if Getting Messy is hard, know that Getting Clear is just around the corner. If taking action is overwhelming, remember that you only have to take one step at a time. If you feel uncomfortable with one of the exercises, trust that another one is on the way. Do one part, take one small action, look at one tiny area for change at a time. You'll be surprised by how much a tiny step forward can affect everything—and how little momentum you need to keep pushing ahead with it.

Fight back against your impulse to settle for a life full of agonizing what-ifs. Fight back against the fear of what you might find on the other side of your mess. On the other side of fear is hope. And just beyond that hope is the change you've been searching for.

If you've ever thought, *It's over. I'm done.* Or, *I can't do this anymore* . . .

If you've ever made pros and cons lists about a job or relationship . . .

INTRODUCTION

If you've ever lain awake at night as the questions swirled but brought you no closer to resolution . . . trust that this practice is designed to turn these painful experiences into tools for self-discovery, clarity, and *action*.

Trust that what you really, really want is already inside you, simply waiting to be unlocked.

PART 1

GET MESSY

Getting Messy is a practice of permission—permission to create space for messiness in our lives. From an early age, we're taught to color inside the lines and keep things tidy and orderly to survive and thrive in a chaotic world. Getting Messy is the playful, "let loose" part of the Life Brief practice. I liken it to a child playing freely in the mud. Let yourself explore, imagine, sling ideas, and reframe your world.

So, clear some space—a table, a spot on the floor, whatever you need. Put on your favorite sweatpants. Pour your beverage of choice. Do whatever you need to do to get comfortable so that you can step into the playground and relish the mud.

The exercises in this part of the book are designed to help you identify and gather the unique "threads" of your life—your values, beliefs, dreams, and desires—so that later in the book, you can distill your Life Brief down to its sharpest and boldest expression.

If one technique doesn't work for you, try another. As you move through this part of the book, keep a pen and a notebook close for moments when inspiration strikes.

Most importantly, trust that the messiness will give way to meaning and bring you closer to a life that is uniquely yours.

CHAPTER 1

SITTING WITH THE MESS

I am ready to . . . drop into myself.

The question: Where do I start?

The practice: Surrender to your fear.

The action: Find Your Quiet.

That long night in my childhood bedroom was my moment to get the chaos out of my brain and onto the page.

I cried and I wrote. I scribbled and underlined, tore out pages, and kept writing. After an hour, I was exhausted, but had a confident feeling that this was the first step. I had to sit in my mess, without avoiding or denying it, in order to gain clarity on what I really wanted . . . what mattered most.

Practicality be damned; fear be double damned. The only way through the misery was to be uncompromisingly honest with myself, without putting boundaries on my needs. What could my life look like if I stopped dictating what was unrealistic or impossible before I'd even tried it? What could my future look like if I dared to admit what I wanted and needed without fear or shame?

I had placed boundaries on my life based on beliefs that Chip didn't want the same things I did, that we were tethered to our existing way of life, that I could only do my job the way it had always been done by others before me, with no room to consider anything different.

But were these beliefs real? Or had my fear dreamed them up?

Many of us are hostages to fear. It's one of our primary boundaries, what holds us back from the life we want. We fear change. We fear disappointing others or ourselves. We fear that the answers to our own questions will create disruption from which we will never recover.

Fear limits the possibilities of alternative stories and outcomes. It makes the path forward seem impossibly narrow, our lives and worlds oppressively small.

Yet getting curious about the fear is the fastest way to unshackle its binds. Accepting, embracing, and reflecting on it—rather than denying or running from it—allows life to unfold in unexpected and unimaginable new ways.

So, I faced my fears head-on. The scary stuff came out first, the anxious stories and raw emotion: fears about the way I'd shut Chip out when I was stressed, anger at how little control I seemed to have over my life and my time.

This isn't working.

Our family is going to fracture and fall apart.

I've pushed him away one too many times to ever bring him back.

Then out came a lot of "if only" dreams—followed quickly by the reasons they could never happen.

If only I could quit my job and have more time with the kids. But we'll be forced to sell the house and ask our parents for support.

If only we could move somewhere more affordable. But Chip will never go for it—he loves our community, as do I. Besides, the agency will never allow it. On and on I went, until I ran out of worries and worst-case scenarios. After I put my pen down and took a deep breath, I felt something I hadn't felt in a while.

I felt *space*.

Something fascinating happens when you face your deep fears and intense emotions—when you bring them out of your mind and onto the page. You see them for what they are: stories that are often distorted or disconnected from reality. Capturing them on the page somehow took their power away.

Not only that. I'd cleared up space in my mind for something else I hadn't felt in a long time—curiosity.

It was then I asked myself: *What if I could live my life in line with what matters most to me?* And almost immediately, another question arose: *Do I even know what matters most to me?*

I didn't, not at first. No words came. But when I asked myself again, I found they wouldn't stop.

I scribbled furiously across the page, rewriting words and adding new phrases. *What do I really want?* That was the insistent question driving my mind. In my heart of hearts, what do I really, really want? I vomited every feeling out onto the page.

I'm not sure how much time passed. I was too swept up in the writing. But at a certain point, I dropped my pen, and that's when I knew I was done.

I was empty—but in a good way, the way you feel after a challenging hike or after sitting down to a meal you've spent all day cooking. I'd let it all out. And when I read through my scribbles, an insight and pattern surfaced—a linchpin to everything I craved . . . the gulf standing between me and all that mattered most in my life, at that moment. What kept coming up, emerging as a theme, and the missing link across everything I longed for—written in various angles on the page, in letters big and small, underlined, and circled—was

TIME

Here's what I ended up with, the five things I allowed myself to admit that I wanted.

THE ORIGINAL LIFE BRIEF:

WHAT I REALLY, REALLY WANT

- Time with my kids, my husband, and for myself
- Time to lean into work that fulfills my unique strengths and gifts
- Time to create an inspiring and loving home for our growing family
- Time to travel and expose our family to the many facets of humanity
- Time to actively participate in a community that shares our values

---

I looked down at this list, exhausted yet elated.

I had done what had seemed impossible for so long: I had turned my agitation, frustration, and despair into a clear and tangible portrait of the life I wanted and needed. More critically, it was a bare, honest declaration, to myself, of what mattered to me and only me.

I sat back and studied the words I'd scrawled on the page. Two realizations came to me. The first was that the stress and terror I felt over the decline in my marriage could be a symptom of something far less severe than the story I was telling myself. I had been gripped by anxiety that I'd married the wrong person and that we were incapable of building a satisfying life together. But when I finally allowed myself to examine the strife surrounding my marriage, I saw something extraordinary. My Life Brief was telling me a different story than my fear had been telling me for so long.

In my heart, I was craving more time with my husband. But not just more time—more *meaningful* time. My Brief cut away the assumptions that my marriage was in trouble and redirected my focus to *how I spend my time.*

The second realization was that what I wanted most was neither extravagant nor extreme. My desire for more time was stunningly simple. Yet, it was out of my immediate grasp.

The art of the Life Brief is to cut away things that are misleading or distracting—doubts, drama, thoughts, and fears that weigh us down, fail to inspire, or detract from the essence of what matters most. When you cut that away, you create a clearing, so that you can zero in and redirect your mind, center your heart, and focus your attention. It's here in this place where clarity appears, and change begins. Shining a light on what's essential puts you on the path towards your unadulterated, most audacious vision.

The Life Brief becomes your constant reminder of that vision, easy to remember because it's sharp and sticky and motivating. It's a key that unlocks new ways of seeing your life, your relationships, your work, yourself. Once you learn to see your world and your choices through the lens of the Life Brief, it's hard to unsee. And that's when everything shifts—your attention, your decisions, your words, your actions.

My first Life Brief was the widest brief I've ever written. It captured everything I needed in my life at that moment in big strokes. I typed up my Brief and texted it to Chip explaining what I'd gone through, how I felt.

Seconds after I sent the text, it hit me that I hadn't texted or called him yet on this trip. Years ago, that would have been unthinkable—but now it was just par for the course to go long stretches without really communicating.

I felt a flood of fear coming back. It was after midnight by that point. He was probably already asleep, and when he woke up, there would be three kids who needed to be dressed, fed, and whisked off to school. No way was he going to be in the headspace for this . . .

Just as I started to doubt what would happen next, I saw those three dots on my phone turn into three letters, all caps, followed by three exclamation marks.

YES!!!

He'd read the Life Brief and resoundingly agreed. What a high, after months of struggle and fighting, cold silences, and unrelenting stress. A simple all-caps, triple-exclamation-mark "yes." This moment of confirmation and alliance was a spark of hope for me—for us.

Of course, practical concerns flooded in right away. How would we go about making this our life? The Life Brief wasn't a bucket list. It was fundamental and urgent. It couldn't wait for the next promotion, the next big client, or the next birthday—we needed to start now.

Then the phone rang. It was him. Soon, we were having the first heart-to-heart we'd had in ages. What I remember most about that conversation is the purity of aliveness and desire to connect—a sense of electricity we hadn't felt during the long winter of our cold spell. It was as if we had both come out of hibernation.

And though there were hundreds of miles between us, I felt right there with my husband for the first time in months. Where there had been silence, suddenly, we were both teeming with eagerness. I could hear the crack in his voice that told me how much this mattered to him. His voice was deep and resonant as he shared his dreams about the kind of community we could participate in or create, the kind of school he hoped to find for our kids—you know, the way people speak when heart and voice are aligned.

Right there on the phone, sometime between two and three in the morning, we made each other two promises: first, that we would be willing to move our family if we needed to; second, that we wouldn't let our fears about money—or, more specifically, the lack thereof—scare us off from making change.

This first Life Brief inspired us to go "off-road" from society's definitions of a "good life" to carve our own path. Once we realized we *could* reconceive our priorities and agreed that we *would* reorganize our lives with our Brief at the center, we became united and energized in a way we had not previously experienced in our marriage. And after that night, when either of us became deflated or flirted with defeat (which definitely happened), we would remind each other, in just a couple words, of our first Life Brief: "Take Our Time."

Those simple words, "Take Our Time," helped us return to our vision whenever we needed. It was a shorthand to remind ourselves and each other of the life we wanted to build for ourselves and our kids. It gave us a way to organize and prioritize our choices and actions. More importantly, the alignment between us redirected our attention away from our critiques about each other, and towards a united view of the life we were energized to create for our family and future.

Our attention shifted away from the usual distractions, and we spent our small slivers of free time trying on ideas, energized by our newfound clarity and alignment. With our sights set on making changes that would allow us the time we needed, I felt a sudden freedom to consider options and opportunities that had never crossed my mind as possibilities.

Without that tear- and snot-stained first Life Brief, I would have never dared to imagine what else our lives could be. I would have told myself, *No, it's unrealistic*, or talked myself out of taking a leap. Many Life Briefs (and moves!) later, the Life Brief has become my central decision-making and life manifestation method.

The Life Brief is your chance to think beyond *how things are* and give space to explore *how you want them to be*. I encourage you to put nothing short of your everything into your Life Brief—to fully embrace how messy it can get. This book is meant to be handled and dog-eared. Stains from your wineglass or coffee mug will dot the pages. Highlight, take notes, and scribble in the columns. Keep it with you wherever you need it, until you realize you are actively living it.

This is your moment to start seeing differently, so that you can start acting differently.

That is what creative, courageous living is all about.

Now, if you're ready, I invite you to ease into your Life Brief—with a simple practice that will help you drop into yourself. If the idea of exercises or action steps stresses you out . . . if it feels like homework or busywork—or any kind of work at all—have no fear. This first action isn't *technically* an action at all. Instead, it's permission to *stop* doing.

(Yep, I know. Easier said than done.)

The Action: Find Your Quiet

When I teach workshops, I give people a little plastic red egg of Silly Putty to play with while I speak. Yes, Silly Putty—the kind we played with as kids. I ask them to take the putty into their hands and squeeze it. Warm it up. Feel the sensation of the stretchy, rubbery, doughlike substance running through their fingers.

I do this to get people to drop into the present moment, to let go of their thoughts—the text they just sent, the rent due next month, the decision or deadline fast approaching. There's a science behind this. Tuning in to our physical senses takes us out of our minds and brings us into the moment.

Turning down the volume on the noise that surrounds us and getting present with ourselves is essential to the Life Brief process. Our minds are incredible theaters but also traps, separating us from the life unfolding right in front of us. We live in a time where we could, if we wanted to, avoid all quiet. We doom scroll late into the night and binge-watch early into the morning. The distractions are infinite—we couldn't even get through a fraction of it in a lifetime.

So, before you go any further, close your eyes and take a deep breath. Feel the air enter your nostrils. Follow it as it fills your lungs and inflates your abdomen. Relish the release as it flushes back out of your belly, and out of your body. Repeat again and then once more.

Drop down into the quiet of this moment.

Note: this isn't a formal meditation where you're trying to train the mind to be still. What I mean by "your quiet" are those moments when you are fully present with yourself, when you're not giving your energy to anything or anyone else.

Ask yourself, what does your quiet look like? When and where does it show up? Or, when and where can you create space for it to show up?

For me, it's the twenty minutes I lie in bed before the day begins, luxuriating in my thoughts before I enter the first sprint of the day. Sure, there are emails to answer, lunches to make, a day to plan. But this time has become too valuable for me to give it away—it's when I'm most connected to my creativity, I receive my biggest aha's, land my sharpest ideas, and untangle my trickiest problems. My quiet is my strategic advantage.

CHAPTER 2

WHAT DO I REALLY WANT?

I am ready to . . . live from the inside out.

The question: What do I really want?

The practice: Follow your curiosity.

The action: Daily Brain Dump.

What do you **really** want?

Perhaps this question brings up a messy swirling mix of frustration or a long list of desires without any sense of priority. Perhaps, on hearing this question, your mind goes blank.

Or perhaps you respond to the question as I first did when I turned the Life Brief practice onto myself.

Who cares? It's impossible anyway, so why bother asking?

Whatever your response is, you're not alone. When I first taught the Life Brief to my agency all those years ago, one of our account directors was the first to raise his hand. He was a rising star in the company—confident, clever, charming—and his question reverberated across the room: *What if you've never allowed yourself to ask what you really want?*

Another colleague, nodding, blurted out the follow-up question I now hear most often, one we'll address in this book:

What if you have no idea?

Asking what you want for your life is, for many of us, a dangerous and forbidden act. From childhood, many of us are taught to listen to the voices of others who, intentionally or unintentionally, dictate to us strict and narrow parameters of how success is measured and achieved. We are given an abundance of advice and instructions for how to navigate the world—so long as we follow a proven path. In school, we're taught to listen to the voices of the people who create the curriculum and hold them as authorities of truth. We're graded not only on our academic achievements but also on our ability to play by the rules and excel at a narrow set of standardized terms.

Some of us struggle less with the question of what we want and more with a sense of helplessness about our ability to get it. Past promises of the American Dream are increasingly out of reach for most people. The wealth, health, and education gaps keep growing, and the metrics of marriage, house, and kids as the only data points that measure success feel increasingly outdated. Faced with disillusionment, many people are asking existential questions like, *Whose life am I living? Are those really the measures I should be using to evaluate my life?* And yes, more people than ever are asking themselves, *What do I really want?*

Regardless of whether you've been questioning societal definitions of happiness for years or have only just begun, the power of the Life Brief is that it challenges the norms that are creating friction in your life. When you have the clarity of a Life Brief, the world no longer feels defined by binaries or standards that simply do not apply to you. I'm writing this book at a time when many people are embracing openness and fluidity at work, in their relationships, and in the way they express their identities. Many are writing their own rules, with a swelling impulse to swerve from the status quo.

And yet, even despite the revolutionary shifts happening across society—many of which are positive, while others are reactionary and limiting—we still lack a common or accepted language for exploring our internal experiences, desires, and needs. Getting in touch with these internal truths is not something many of us have been encouraged to do. Too often, our deeper desires get masked by the trappings of conventionality—we strive towards milestones other people have laid out, rather than following our curiosity and mapping a course towards what we desire from the depths of our being.

The Life Brief gives you a chance to take a step back to look at the whole map and ask whether the course you're following is leading you to a destination you actually want to reach. It's a practice in what I call "living from the inside out." Inside-out living requires steady engagement from you. We achieve it only when we get curious about our own voices and innermost desires.

Many of us are living from the outside in: listening to and living by advice from other people's voices—be it friends, family, or culture at large—voices that tell us, *This is what you should want.* Outside-in living happens when we follow rules and expectations set by others because it's either what we've been conditioned to do or what we feel pressured to do.

In his book *The Second Mountain*, David Brooks calls this climbing "the first mountain"—get a good education, embark on a lifelong career, find the right life partner, and then you'll know success. The problem with first mountain living, Brooks argues, is that many people reach the top only to experience emptiness or a subtle yet palpable hum of restlessness. Others never reach the peak, knocked off the first mountain by tragedy or loss, finding themselves in a valley of dismay or despair. It's from one of these two places—the empty peak or the valley of despair—where some people strike out on a new climb. From the foothills of a second mountain, they embark on a journey through uncharted terrain in search of inner joy versus the outer-directed happiness they were once sold.

The Life Brief is designed to be a guide on the journey up the "second mountain"—a mountain of our own making, on a horizon we envision by and for ourselves.

I want to be clear. This isn't a choice between an easy path and a harder one. Both outside-in and inside-out living require showing up. They both require continual engagement, dedication, and resilience. But on the outside-in path, people are often left feeling a void even after they've received, achieved, and checked every box. Like I did, they may experience a sense of disconnect: Their lives look great on paper, so why doesn't it feel like a happy ending? They've followed the path to success step by step, so why are they exhausted in a way that feels lifeless, stale, or wrung-out empty? That hum of residual restlessness continues to re-verberate after the high of each new achievement fades. After reflecting on life before their first Life Brief session, people often tell me that they thought, *Was that it? Okay, well, what's next?* Box-checking is its own blind obsession. Yet a vacuum remains, whether big or small.

Learning to live from the inside out frees us from the map that was handed to us by the outside world. You will still experience exhaustion on the second mountain—but there's a satisfaction at the end of each day because you're working in service of something deeper. You are being guided by your own compass, your goals generated from within, and your destination created for you alone. There's a glow that's bigger and beyond ego.

I call this invigorating feeling *soul-spent satisfied.*

As you Get Messy, you may start to reconsider some of the goals and milestones you've been chasing. You may realize that you have been following a path or checklist that is not actually aligned with your values, beliefs, or desires. You might identify interests and desires that have gone dormant. As you give yourself permission to consider (or reconsider) what it is that you truly want, you might realize that those things are not a part of your current daily life.

The Life Brief is a practice of turning over untouched stones and examining what's beneath. It challenges you to ask questions for which your own answers might scare or surprise you. You might get disappointed. You might get uncomfortable. You might get frustrated that you've been misdirecting your attention, time, or energy. If this happens to you, keep going. I promise that your second mountain is right around the corner—and that the rewards for that climb are worth it.

In teaching the Life Brief, I've met a lot of people undergoing a reckoning about how much of their lives have been spent scaling the first mountain.

I've come to see it in people's eyes—a kind of eagerness, like there's something inside that they can't hold back anymore. I saw that look in my friend Marcus's eyes when I bumped into him at a restaurant not long after I'd begun teaching the Life Brief. When I asked how he was doing, he didn't respond with the usual polite script. Instead, he leapt at the chance to have a sounding board for how unsatisfied he was with his career, how ready he was for a change.

What came out in that first interaction was the immense *pressure* that weighed on Marcus. For all their support and good intentions, his family had ingrained in him a conventional definition of material and career success—a growing bank account, impressive house, enviable title. Adding to the pressure, his brothers embodied this classic portrait of success, leaving Marcus feeling like he was floundering in comparison.

His career had been paved with a series of corporate marketing jobs carrying titles that signaled his ascension on the first mountain. But he felt unfulfilled by the nature of these roles, the pace of the work, the constant pressure to conform to stiff and stifling cultures. His discontent revealed itself in different ways, eventually leading Marcus to either quit each role or be laid off. As a result, he was frequently "in between jobs."

Yet with every new job search Marcus found himself chasing similar roles as he had held before. He wasn't exactly excited about these new opportunities, but he couldn't see any alternatives.

We decided that instead of focusing on his professional title, as he had done in past goal-setting exercises, he would instead zero in on the kind of *experience* he wanted from his work. *What kinds of people, interactions, and cultures feed and fuel me? How do I want to feel in my workdays? How do I want to show up? How do I want to be received? What role do I want my work to play in my life beyond the paycheck?*

I suggested one of my go-to strategy techniques. We identified some "taboo words" and themes—those that have become habitual yet bankrupt of meaning. For an internet company, a taboo word might be "speed." Every internet company needs to provide speed—it's no longer a real point of differentiation. We need to go deeper.

By coming up with taboo themes tailored to Marcus's situation, we created constraints to help him think differently about his work. When asking himself what he really wanted out of his career, he was pushed to think beyond "money," "job title," or "company names."

Only after we took those words and themes off the table did Marcus realize just how fixated he'd been on big titles and companies with elite reputations, and how little thought he'd given to the impact a company's culture would have on his day-to-day satisfaction.

The exercises in *The Life Brief* are designed to trigger these kinds of realizations in our writing and reflections. They also invite us to show up differently almost immediately—to bring new levels of curiosity to every interaction.

I was driving one day when Marcus called to share an experience unlike others he'd had in the past. I could hear excitement in his voice: he talked fast but was centered and calm. I'd not heard this level of glow from him before.

He'd just been to a sales convention. He had spent a couple of hours working at his company's booth. Though he'd met a lot of people during the convention, two conversations stood out—one with the owner of a sales franchise, and the other with a woman who was head of marketing at a larger organization. He was moved by the depth and vulnerability in these conversations, a level that he had not experienced before in a "business" setting.

"What was it about these conversations that got you so energized?" I asked.

"They were *curious* about me—my ideas and my take on their businesses," he explained.

Both genuinely wanted Marcus's opinion about how their brands were being expressed creatively. As I listened to him speak, the word that kept coming up time and again was "creativity."

No wonder his previous jobs had ended in disappointment. Not only had his roles been predominantly strategic or analytic, but many of the companies he had worked for were known for their cutthroat cultures and high turnover.

What Marcus realized was that he wanted a role at a creative-at-heart company where he could bring the full force of his creative spirit. He also wanted a work environment with *other* creative spirits. He was most alive when working in a company that valued emotional intelligence as much as IQ. He called his Life Brief "Creative at Heart," a sticky description of the type of company, role, and experience he was seeking.

With a newly sharpened focus, Marcus committed to his job search with an inside-out mindset. He sought out opportunities with companies across a wide variety of industries and changed his approach to interviews, approaching them from a place of curiosity. Rather than see them as "tests" in which he could prove his knowledge, he used them as conversations to determine whether they'd offer him the experience he really wanted. He paid attention to the kind of work and work experience that would satisfy his desire for creativity and self-governance. He even turned down a couple of seemingly impressive opportunities when they failed to align with his Brief.

Several months into his search, he landed a leadership role overseeing a dynamic creative team at a fast-growing company. It was in an industry he would have never considered before, but the company's culture was too vibrant to pass up. He was relieved, gratified, and genuinely energized in his new role.

A few months into this job, Marcus's company put out a search for a chief marketing officer, a position much like the ones he had previously aspired to hold. Marcus immediately put himself up for the job—reflexively responding to old beliefs that promotions and title bumps were the metrics of success that mattered most. But as the hiring process progressed, he began to realize that the role he already occupied *was* the job he had described in his Work Brief, a role that left him feeling invigorated and alive at the end of each day.

The urge to chase conventional success—that "first mountain success"—can be hard to shake. It can be so deeply ingrained in us that it's hard to see, much less resist. As soon as Marcus realized this, he knew that the CMO position would be a mistake—he would be leaving a role he loved to go back to a pattern that had perpetually failed to satisfy him. He rescinded his application and leaned wholeheartedly into the job he already had. Seeing his confidence in his role, his company expanded and elevated his position, giving him more freedom and opportunity to do what he loved.

He recently shared with me a video of his opening remarks to his team of eighty-five people—a talk in which he invited and encouraged them to bring more boldness and vulnerability to their work. What I witnessed in him was clarity, strength, emotional intelligence—traits of high-performing leaders.

Marcus's story is about the unexpected rewards that reveal themselves when we shift from outside-in to inside-out living. But how do we make such a profound shift in the way we see the world—and our place in it?

What I've discovered is that the shortest path to inner-directed living is to start with questions, not answers.

Allow your curiosity to lead the way forward. When we lean into our curiosity, we unlock insights and epiphanies about what makes our lives worth living. In my experience, that exploration often reveals latent, buried, or previously undiscovered paths for living that transform overwhelm into adventure. It liberates us from restless striving, reaching for goals and lifestyles that leave us accomplished yet unfulfilled. As I have learned over the years, *How can I have it all?* is a misleading question. The real question is, *How can I have all that matters?*

At the start of every workshop I've taught, over the span of many years, I've watched people experience the torrent of doubt that comes with trying something new. Let me assure you of this: opening up to curiosity takes the panic out of this practice. Because as soon as we tune into our innate curiosity, we break down the overwhelm and redirect our attention to the joy of discovery.

It may take practice to get into the habit of regular self-inquiry. Anyone who has spent time around young kids has witnessed their innate curiosity. But studies show that once kids begin school, the rate of question asking drops significantly. Evidence suggests that asking questions is a natural, biological instinct, one that falls off as we grow up. In order to unlock your Life Brief, you'll need to reactivate your curiosity instinct.

This commitment to curiosity is well worth it. Questions have a way of short-circuiting self-doubt, comparison, and anxious thoughts by directing our attention to something more productive—our hunt for answers.

When your brain is searching for the answer to a question, it can't think of anything else. According to David Hoffeld, author of *The Science of Selling*, this is a reflex known as "instinctive elaboration." If you give yourself over to the question "what do I want?" your brain is too busy to get distracted by other questions, such as "what if I don't get there?" "how could I ever do that?" or other reasons that what you want can't happen. In this way, curiosity can be an antidote to anxiety.

Questions also stimulate intimacy—not only with others but also with ourselves. They reveal insights and aha's we had not considered before, bringing us closer to understanding ourselves and those around us.

The answers we seek lie in the questions we avoid.

The type of questions we ask matter. A strategist's job is to ask what I call *penetrating questions*—incisive questions that dig deep and unlock fast. They're questions that are hard to hide from. *What do you really want?* is one of my favorites because it cuts right through the bullshit. *How do you want to be remembered?* is another.

The goal of penetrating questions isn't always to acquire clear answers. Questions also help us plumb the depths, to shake up inner truths that we've locked in the vault.

What happens *after* we ask questions also matters. It's important to take the time to reflect. As philosopher and education reformer John Dewey said, "We do not learn from experience. We learn from reflecting on experience."

The next practice is designed to ease you into your curiosity—a low-stakes, judgment-free way to connect to your inner voice. We're going to commit to a short daily writing practice to get closer to your answer to that question, *What do I really want?*—making space each day to be honest, unfiltered, and raw.

The Action: Daily Brain Dump

It's hard to create space for possibility when that space is crowded by to-do lists, worries, or old, dusty narratives. We need to start clearing out the clutter!

We do it with a Daily Brain Dump.

A few minutes of writing every day not only helps us surface what we want and what matters most in our lives, but it also helps us clue in on beliefs and stories that are holding us back. I call the recurring words, themes, and phrases that show up in our Brain Dumps "threads." In part 2, we'll see how seemingly disconnected ideas come together to weave a unique tapestry that serves as the basis of our Life Briefs.

But for now, all we need to do is clear out the clutter. The Daily Brain Dump is not a one-time exercise. It is a daily practice that gets you accustomed to using curiosity as a way to deepen your relationship with yourself over time.

The pace is yours. The space is yours. The pen is yours. Allow it to lead. There is no planning required or editing allowed. This exercise is designed to allow your thoughts and feelings, whatever they might be, to come through you, out of you, and onto the page. This is a practice in curiosity and non-judgment. This is a practice of privacy and permission. You're not writing for anybody else. Nobody's watching, so go for it.

There may be times when you find yourself stuck or critical of what comes out. Keep going. Don't edit or judge yourself. Just let it out. In this exercise, writing acts as a cathartic release. The act of unearthing, even if you never read it again, allows for physical embodiment and growth.

This is also an opportunity to capture your aha's and park your doubts. Doubts are indications of lurking limiting narratives cluttering your mind. This is the place to get out thoughts like, *This is bullshit. This is uncomfortable. I'm not going to get anything out of it.* Once they leave your mind, you open up space for new thoughts, ideas, and possibilities to enter.

Dumping my unfiltered thoughts on the page was the very first step I took in my own Life Brief—and it remains a practice that keeps me centered and self-directed. The Daily Brain Dump is where you begin.

Start your Daily Brain Dump and commit to it for (at least) two weeks:

1. **Grab a piece of paper and a pen.** Ideally, you're going analog, using real paper and not your phone or computer. Set a timer for 10 minutes.
2. **Write.** Capture everything that comes to mind. Get it all out onto the page. Write fast and write furiously, without judgment, withholding, or self-censorship.
3. **Anything goes**—big stuff, little stuff, random stuff. Drawings, diagrams, and doodles are all allowed and encouraged. If you ever get stuck, bring your mind back to answering, "What do I *really* want?"

As you delve into this daily practice, you may start to notice patterns or insights about yourself or your situation. I invite you to dedicate a separate space in your notebook to create a running list of aha's that emerge along the way. We'll come back to what to do with that list in part 2—for now, all you need to do is write. Go ahead. Do it now. There's no better time. The rest will wait.

CHAPTER 3

REARRANGE THE FURNITURE

I am ready to . . . listen to the answers that emerge.

The question: What's beneath the surface?
The practice: Allow your answers to find you.
The action: Let Your Pen Lead.

Be honest with me. Did you skip—or were you tempted to skip—the Daily Brain Dump? Do you doubt that scribbling a few words each day could actually lead to anything *that* game-changing?

I know many people who resist writing. Heck, I'm one of them. Either we don't consider ourselves writers or have little interest in making writing a part of our lives. Or maybe you *are* a writer, but feel that you've been here, done this before. Perhaps you've got a pile of unfinished notebooks and planners collecting dust—once a faithful explorer of your inner world, without much change to show for it.

I get it. I really do. I have never thought of myself as a writer, not in the long form, at least. Never did I imagine writing a book. My resistance to writing has me procrastinating until the very last minute. In fact, I'm late getting this manuscript back to my editor as I type these very words!

But writing is essential to the Life Brief for good reason.

Neurophysiologists have shown that writing ideas down by hand—as opposed to just ruminating on them or even typing them—opens up cognitive capacity. We remember concepts better when we feel physical feedback from the pressure of our pen on the page. We're more creative when we scribble, cross out, underline.

"Writing rearranges the furniture of our minds," says poet Roger Housden. The act of putting pen to paper stirs up and moves around what's inside, allowing us to see how different arrangements of ideas resonate within.

Strategists use writing exercises, prompts, and drawings when interviewing people for research. These exercises unlock and unearth truths when we have limited pockets of time. They help people break from rote answers and scripted stories when asked about their perceptions, decisions, and behaviors.

Just as it's a strategist's job to search for the riches that make each company or brand unique, the Life Brief deputizes you to become the strategist of your own life, empowering *you* to move things around in your mind, try new ideas on for size, and explore new possibilities.

Find Your Quiet and the Brain Dump are the first steps in clearing the clutter of our minds—they will become indispensable parts of your housecleaning repertoire. But as anyone who's ever cleaned their house knows, to really make things sparkle, you have to do some heavy lifting. You have to push the furniture around if you want to get into those tough-to-reach nooks and crannies.

Rearranging the furniture of our minds is about getting beyond the scripted stories that we tell ourselves and others. It's about taking a deep look behind and underneath our mental and emotional furniture for hidden truths. By rearranging this old furniture—or putting it out on the curb altogether—we unlock new pathways for creative living.

One of my first Life Brief workshops was attended by a young woman named Regan. Regan lit up every room with her laughter and ideas. She was bright, conversational, and moved with a magnetism that made others take notice. She was a regular at company events—softball games, trivia nights, team picnics, and parties. Everyone knew her and loved being around her. On the outside, she was "the life of the party." But inside, Regan was wrestling with demons.

During the workshop, she was the first to raise her hand and ask, "Where do you start if you have no idea of what you want?" It was a simple, yet brave, question that paved the way for others thinking the same. Yet Regan would later tell me that speaking up left her feeling embarrassed and exposed, scared that she had put something into the universe that she wasn't ready for.

It was as if she had "let the genie out of the bottle," she later shared. Though she didn't talk about it that day, she had written something in one of her first Life Brief exercises that had shaken her up, hooked into her, and stayed with her long after the workshop.

"Do I have a drinking problem?" Followed by, "Doesn't everyone have a drinking problem?"

It wasn't the first time Regan had asked herself about her relationship with alcohol—wasn't the first time she wondered if her drinking was "normal"—but for a long time, each time the thought surfaced, she batted it away.

She'd do the same after that first Life Brief workshop: tuck her suspicions about drinking into a corner where she wouldn't have to see them. Then she turned her attention outward: to her career. She craved a bigger role with more challenging responsibilities—and now that she had declared it on the page, she felt ready to mobilize and turn this goal into reality. Her first Life Brief helped her to push aside stories about her lack of experience, credibility, or readiness to level up. With a clear Life Brief in mind of what she wanted from her work life, Regan landed a new job within months. She moved to Los Angeles and threw herself into her next chapter.

But though she had rearranged the furniture, the clutter remained. Her drinking was becoming a star player in her life, as much as she tried to hide it in the background. And now that she was alone, away from her family, it came sharply into focus. As she settled into her new surroundings, she understood that part of what had motivated her to move cities and change jobs was an underlying desire to be alone. "Sometimes an animal goes off by itself when it knows it's sick," she told me in reflection. "I think part of me was feeling like *I don't want my family to keep seeing me this way. If I go somewhere where no one that I care about sees me, is that an easier place to suffer?*"

But even though Regan had only moved some of the furniture around in that first Life Brief workshop, she had begun the crucial work of looking within. As Regan achieved the outward desires of her first Life Brief, she simultaneously followed her curiosity about therapy. She found a therapist she liked shortly after moving to LA. In her sessions, she talked about feeling sad and possibly depressed, but avoided any mention of alcohol. Part of her hoped to treat her depression without having to look alcoholism in the eyes. When her therapist prescribed an antidepressant, it came with a warning: "You cannot drink alcohol while taking this medication." Regan agreed, feeling better for having a solution, medication meant to solve her problem right there in the palm of her hand.

Only, she couldn't stop drinking. Regan went home to San Francisco to spend the weekend with her family and attend her nephew's baptism. "I was just wrecked," she says. "Just completely wasted and on this medication, too. I drank a lot of alcohol on it, and my brain lost it. It felt dangerous. I was spiraling. I'd never felt that chemically wrong before. I cried to my family after church. I remember saying, 'It's got me. I'm not me anymore. It got me, and I can't stop drinking. I'm sorry.'

"I put it all out there to the room, to my family. I knew that I wouldn't have said it unless I was that drunk, but in this moment, literally my whole family was around me, and I broke down and told them: 'I can't stop.'" This moment was Regan's rock bottom. She'd laid it all out, bare, on the table to those she loved most. She knew that she couldn't go back from that. Even still, she found herself drinking to the point of inebriation on the flight back home to LA. Her mother flew down the next day, stayed with her for a week, and helped her turn towards a new direction.

Regan's confession to her family meant that she could no longer deny her alcohol abuse. She had gone into therapy thinking she could skirt by—but the very act of avoidance only exposed her alcoholism further. Regan knew she no longer had a choice. She had to quit—she would lose her life if she didn't.

Back in therapy, ready to embrace a deeper level of change, Regan came back to the Life Brief practice—this time ready to focus on the issue that she had not been ready to face the first time through.

She returned to the original question that had set this journey in motion: *What do I really, really want?* In sitting with that question, the Life Brief created a space for Regan to finally explore her relationship with alcohol. She realized she could drink two or three bottles of wine in one sitting, and not even feel drunk. After a long period of introspection, Regan knew it was time to be honest with herself and face whatever answers came out on the page.

She returned to every question around alcohol that had come up in her first Life Brief work.

Doesn't everyone in their twenties have a drinking problem?

Isn't this how young professionals live?

Is the way I drink really that different?

These questions helped her see how much she was drinking, how often—and how much her doubts about her relationship with alcohol were a part of her overall unease about her life.

They also helped her see the chaos that drinking was creating in her life. She thought back to breaking down in front of her family, to how often she felt as if she was living in a fog.

Was this what she *really* wanted?

The desire for sobriety gave Regan a newfound clarity which helped her as she continued the Life Brief practice. In the coming chapters, we'll explore how to bring our inner and outer selves into greater alignment—a part of the journey that proved revelatory for Regan. What she would discover as she began that deeper level of inquiry was that she wasn't as extroverted as she believed. Underneath her "life of the party" façade, she was gripped by social anxiety, and had long been using alcohol to bolster her confidence.

She could see that she was living out some long-held limiting beliefs as her truths:

Wasn't it "party Regan" who got all the attention and interest from people?

There's no way sober Regan could be as interesting, cool, or fun.

"I thought that alcohol added to my personality, and it didn't," she told me. "It was holding me back, so much so that I couldn't be in a room without it."

As the fog cleared, she began to recall the times that others expressed their concern about her drinking—and how she had been unable to hear them. She realized that change could not be activated until she wanted it, deep in her bones.

"People had been telling me I had a problem, but I didn't listen," she said. "It didn't matter until I felt it, until I *wanted* to face it. Sometimes you have to sit with how much something hurts, then get to the point where you can't take it anymore before you can find your way out of it."

The Life Brief gave Regan a safe place to ask the question that un-locked it all, even though she couldn't see where it was going until she arrived. The more she uncovered, the more she was able to face that which she had previously skirted and suppressed—a truth she knew was beckoning but she actively ignored: that alcoholism and the persona that went with it wasn't the person she was or wanted to be. This aha moment was the first step to her sobriety, and now, she's been sober for many years.

When we let ourselves write—write freely without fear—we invite the unconscious forward, moving beyond our "scripts" into our truth. Writing is the key. Simply thinking through our issues is too vague, too noncommittal. Like waves in the ocean, one thought gets washed away by another. Connections between how we're currently living and what we really want can be fleeting, easily lost if not captured. Writing commits our thoughts and feelings to paper so that we can be in a relationship with them and with ourselves—artifacts of our interior available for reflection, refinement, and re-imagining.

The exercise below invites you to write without plan. It is designed to surface things from our subconscious and lay them bare on the page for us to receive and reflect on. That's the journey of rearranging the furniture, and it's just one of many tools in the strategist's toolbox. It allows us to discover what's underneath that we might not even be aware of in this moment.

What is it that you really want that you're afraid to admit? That is the question we're going to lean into, to stir up, uncover, and rearrange the furniture of your deepest desires.

I speak a lot about giving ourselves permission to write boldly and bravely as part of the Life Brief practice. I want to be clear that in stepping bravely into that permission, your Life Brief writing could—and probably should—get uncomfortable, ugly even.

I remember vividly a woman named Barbara who attended a Life Brief workshop. She loudly declared that she was sick and tired of being a people pleaser. "Even my journal entries are nice!" she said. "Anytime someone wrongs me, I'll first see it from their side before I even acknowledge that I've been hurt."

I've met others who've shared similar experiences—people whose reflex is to move into peacemaking mode before they've acknowledged their own feelings. This can lead to making life choices that prioritize other people's expectations over your own desires, suppressing your own needs—sometimes without you even noticing that it's happening. The power of penetrating questions is that they help us move past the politeness so we can get the mess out. Consider these questions:

If your tears could talk, what would they say?

What are you denying yourself?

What would you declare if you stopped denying yourself?

When Barbara asked herself these kinds of questions—and when she allowed herself to answer in naked honesty—a new level of understanding opened up for her. The practice helped her admit that she wasn't ready to forgive an ex who had cheated on her and lied to her for months. In fact, she realized that she no longer gave a shit about his point of view. Maybe someday she would forgive him, but she wasn't ready yet. And that's the truth about what she really wanted—to not have to accept her ex-boyfriend's (or anyone else's) poor treatment.

When I encourage you to write without judgment, I really mean *no* judgment. Sometimes you need to write into the pain, the self-pity, and all the other places that polite society would not have us go. In an early Brain Dump leading up to one of my Marriage Briefs, I wrote the words: "I want to burn it all down." Those are terrifying words to read on a page, but it was a release of raw honesty that I desperately needed at that moment when I felt the weight of the world on my shoulders. Give yourself permission to go there. If it helps, tell yourself that the second after you let yourself write the words, you can rip them up, burn them, or flush them down the toilet.

While I encourage you to keep all of your writing until part 2 so you can reflect upon what has come up, paper is mercifully fragile. If you need to get out something ugly and brutal to clear your mind, you can always take note of the "safer" highlights and set flame to the rest.

The Action: Let Your Pen Lead

Whereas our Daily Brain Dump was our warm-up writing exercise—a gentle immersion into the practice of non-judgment—we're now going to use a targeted creative prompt to help us go deeper. And we're going to nudge ourselves to write for longer.

We're officially moving into the realm of the subconscious, much like André Breton, a founding member of the Surrealists, did with his practice of automatic writing.

Find a comfortable and quiet place to drop into writing.

Set a timer for 20 to 30 minutes.

Have plenty of paper at hand—a notebook is best.

The goal of this practice is to write continuously for the entire time, without pause.

Start by writing the following sentence at the top of your page:

In my heart of hearts,
what I really want but am afraid to admit, is . . .

Yes, we're returning to that same vital question—*What do you really want?*—but we're adding a new layer this time. By acknowledging how hard it is to admit to what we *really* want, we're giving ourselves permission to go to the places that might not just feel scary or impossible, but also those that thrill us so much that they feel a little dangerous.

Finish the sentence in your own words and continue from there until the timer rings. Every time your pen stalls, look at the top of the page and begin the sentence again.

Do not stop writing, even if you run out of things to write. If needed, you can write "I don't know what to write" over and over until something else surfaces.

Don't jump to the practical side of things like how much would need to change or what else you would need to do to make what you really want a reality. Just allow these natural inspirations to bubble up from within.

What are you holding inside that's ready to get out?

CHAPTER 4

CLOSE THE GAP

I am ready to . . . stop hiding.

The question: Who am I, really?
The practice: Reconnect with the real you.
The action: Look Behind the Mask.

My father was a booming dinner table presence. My most vivid memories are of him, a tumbler of Seagram's Seven Crown over ice in one hand and a Marlboro Red in the other, telling tales of fleeing China during the Cultural Revolution—always on the run or hiding from capture.

As a child, I was captivated by these stories. The stories of my grandparents escaping imprisonment, dodging threats, and overcoming hardships took on the outsized qualities of myths, lined with morals about courage and justice. In school, I found myself drawn to, and eventually obsessed with, Helen Keller, Amelia Earhart, and Martin Luther King Jr., historical figures who overcame inconceivable obstacles. A fascination grew inside me: What makes some people brave hardships no one else would dare to take on? And, more personally, how can I muster that bravery in the face of my own struggles?

My family immigrated from Taiwan to California when I was six years old. I remember being promised a child's version of the American Dream—that we were moving to a wonderland where anything could happen. I recall my mom and grandma taking me to the circus in Taipei, telling me that America was just as marvelous, maybe better.

The reality was, let's say, a little different. In Los Angeles, our suburban neighborhood was middle-class and predominantly white. For years growing up, I was the shy bucktoothed Asian girl among a sea of white faces. In the fourth grade, my brother and I started walking home together after school, latchkey kids who had to look out for one another. By then, I'd grown used to people who made me feel like I didn't belong. While I could shrug off insults directed at me, the sting of watching my brother get hurt was achingly intolerable.

Three years younger than me, my brother was the definition of adorable—a round-faced, bright-eyed kid who followed me everywhere. Instead of using my name, he called me *Jiejie*, which in Mandarin means "older sister." After school each day, he'd wait by my classroom door until I was free to walk home. "*Jiejie, jiejie*! Sister, sister!" he would call out to me from the other side of the classroom. "I'm ready!"

That tender memory for me is often shrouded in shame. I wince, even today, when I think back on the way I felt when I heard the other kids break into laughter when they heard him. "Sister, sister!" they mocked. I wasn't so upset about my own humiliation; I was pained on my brother's behalf. Even at eight and nine, I felt a deep responsibility to shield him from such taunting. Sometimes I could. And sometimes, I failed.

One day, a boy ran out of his house and towards us as we were walking home. He started punching my brother in the arm, calling him names. He bombarded us with the slurs I'd already become accustomed to: "Chink!" he yelled. "Go back to your country!" My brother wailed from the shock and pain. I screamed at the bully—a boy from my grade—until he went back into his house. I put my arms around my brother and walked him home in silence, at a loss for how to comfort him.

I held back my own tears until I was safely behind the closed doors of my bedroom. I wouldn't allow myself to cry in front of my brother. This wasn't the first time I'd hidden my tears—I felt I had to be strong to protect and defend both my brother and my mom from my dad's depression-fueled alcoholic rages. I was the only one in the family willing to meet my dad's fury eye to eye.

But on that day, I'd been forced to face a whole other form of fury.

I never forgot the obscenities or the cutting force of those words. That memory, among others like it, was seared into my young soul. It marked my earliest understanding of belonging, of where I stood in relation to the world around me. Incidents like these formed and fueled long-held limiting beliefs that I was not worthy of acceptance. I absorbed these racial slurs (and worse ones) deep into my bones.

The next year, I became friends with the boy who beat on my brother. I wagered that the most effective form of protection from the pain of being "othered" was fitting in—which I later came to understand as assimilation. It was an act of self-preservation, but I never fully trusted our friendship. This became a theme in many of my childhood relationships. The boy's words fed my drive to assimilate and adopt Western beliefs and ways of being while simultaneously rejecting my own culture, confidence, beauty, and body. It took decades for me to unpack and then heal the scars of these slurs. And to be honest, I'm still working on it today.

One day, in the middle of eighth grade, I stood on the blacktop during recess, watching the easy confidence of the other girls, and had an epiphany. My life was mine to make. That recess, I made a decision. I would no longer be that shy outsider. Not in high school—not ever again. This was the first time I got really clear about what I wanted, and many of my choices since then can be traced back to that moment. As I had become a seasoned observer of how middle schoolers socialize, I was struck by an idea. Spending many bored after-school hours at the public library, I had recently come across a book of shockingly dirty jokes—foul stuff, full of sexual innuendo, curse words, and other semiscandalous content. I decided to shake things up on the blacktop. Before long, I was telling jokes surrounded by laughing classmates. I thought, *Whoa, what is happening? How did I find myself in the center of the circle?* I kept up this practice of intentional extraversion, even as it went against my own nature at the time. Soon, throwing myself into situations that simultaneously excited and terrified me became my way of navigating the world.

As for many teens, the urgency of emotional survival was both a catalyst and driver of my adolescence. I equated popularity with protection from pain, and I was determined to have as many friends as possible. In this way, I made my first deliberate outside-in choice—to lose myself in serving other people's needs while disconnecting from my own. I became the go-to party hostess on the weekends, even though I would have preferred simpler, more intimate time with friends. I sold myself as a flirty, fun girl and downplayed my academic prowess and ambitions. I fed friendships that boosted my popularity, letting them slowly overshadow those that enriched my soul.

By the end of high school, my résumé included class president, student body president, and varsity athlete. I was the homecoming princess, prom queen, and student representative to the school board. My house had become weekend party central. By graduation, I had firmly made my way to the inner circle, as far from the outside as humanly possible. But my focused pursuit of belonging as protective armor had its consequences. It got to the point that I struggled to distinguish between real friendships and transactional ones. I found it difficult to discern who I could count on, trust, or turn to for help in times of need. The imprints of rejection clouded my relational judgment, casting long shadows of caution and confusion into my adult life.

Most costly, I distanced myself from anything that signaled my Chineseness. I will never forget my father's searing anger when I begged him to stop speaking Chinese in front of my "friends." Or my mom's pain when I told her I was embarrassed by the smell of her home cooking.

There's a difference between pushing out of our comfort zones because of a deep internal calling, and chasing measures of success fueled by status, envy, or even a sense of safety. We tend to do the latter when we're living *outside-in*, and the former when we're truly living *inside-out*. Remember, inside-out living happens when we're connected to and guided by our own voice, our unique truth, and our innermost desires. Outside-in living happens when we're moved by the voices, actions, or examples of others. The temptations and pressure to live outside-in surround us—in the media, on our social feeds, in our communities. It's captured in our vernacular, "keeping up with the Joneses" or, in this cultural moment, the Kardashians. It happens when we believe that our community's metrics for success are more important than our own sense of fulfillment.

In my adolescence, it was easier to become a new person who checked the boxes of teenage metrics for popularity than it was to make space for the person I longed to become in my heart of hearts. I chose to follow my first mountain desire to be insulated from my outsiderness, the only way I believed I could ever be accepted, liked, or safe. Later in life, it took creativity and courage for me to think beyond those boxes and find a way back to "me." But it was important work for me to do—so important, in fact, that I made a career out of teaching others how to do it for their brands, ideas, and actions.

My job as a strategist is to prevent others from falling into the trap of believing that being like others is the path to success. I help clients define and express their unique magic and run towards that place of distinction. Strategists look for gaps in a brand's perception—a misalignment in who the brand is, or why it exists with people's perceptions of what it stands for. This skewed perception can be the reason why a brand isn't connecting with the audience it seeks. When there's misalignment between who you are and what you convey to the world, it comes at a cost. For companies, the cost may be financial or a blow to their reputation—but with people, the cost is losing touch with who they are.

In her book *Blonde*, novelist Joyce Carol Oates writes about the tragic life of Marilyn Monroe: though she wanted desperately to be seen for who she really was, she lost herself to an audience who couldn't take their eyes off of the manufactured image. Describing the film inspired by her book, Oates writes, "In a sense, Norma Jeane Baker represents the authentic self—as we all possess 'authentic selves' usually hidden beneath layers of defensive personae. 'Marilyn Monroe' is the performing self that exists only when there is an audience."

For Monroe the consequences of this misalignment between her authentic and performing selves were great on every level: emotionally, spiritually, and physically. But even if we've never achieved the same levels of fame or experienced the same public scrutiny, we've likely all experienced how disorienting it can be when these two selves are at odds.

For me, this misalignment meant that I began to chase what I thought would earn me inclusion, respect, and belonging: I became the extrovert, the high achiever, and, later, the successful strategist, the picture-perfect parent and partner. I found it increasingly difficult to determine which relationships existed only because of the mask I wore, and which penetrated to a deeper appreciation for who I was underneath. I had a hard time trusting anyone enough to be able to lean on them, to ask for help, to confide in them. This mistrust left me feeling heavy and isolated, and I struggled to keep moving forward. It became difficult to appreciate or enjoy my day-to-day life or to relish the successes that I fought so hard to win. I had become so accustomed to building protective walls around myself and only showing people what

I thought they wanted to see that I was barring people from access to the most genuine parts of me.

If we never take the time to reflect on whether our inner and outer selves are in alignment, it's easy to fall into "scripts" about who we are and what really matters to us. *I'm the life of the party*, we think. Or *I'm the glue that keeps everyone together . . . the mom of the group . . . the responsible one.*

Maybe these scripts made sense for us once, but if they get out of balance with who we are, the costs can be devastating.

What voices are you carrying in your head that are not your own? What masks have you put on for protection? What scripts are you playing out without asking whether they feel genuine to you?

These questions may be uncomfortable to face. They may be difficult to answer because of how long it's been since you examined your path and reflected about what set you on it. But you're not alone in that discomfort. How often do any of us make space for our voices and true selves to break through? This is your time and invitation to do just that.

The Action: Look Behind the Mask

This exercise is about seeing and embracing the parts of ourselves that we have hidden, shelved, or tucked away because they feel dangerously revealing. It's a practice of deep listening, of allowing your inner voice to rise and guide you forward.

Sometimes we need help clearing away the noise so we can reconnect with our beliefs. The practice of active reflection by way of creative exercises allows us to surface parts of our identity that we might have forgotten or neglected. These exercises allow us to uncover deeper insights and bolder ideas for alternate ways of living and being. They force us to ponder how we actively display our values to the world. *Do* we actively display them to the world?

When we face our agitation instead of avoiding it, we uncover our deepest beliefs. And when we declare those beliefs, we activate ways of being that are more aligned with who we are—the key to "no-regrets living."

1. **Start by making two lists.** The first list represents who you are. How would you describe yourself when you are completely free to be yourself? How would you describe yourself when engaged in the things you love doing? Write for as long as you can, listing everything that comes to mind without judgment or editing.

2. **For the second list,** take note of how other people see or experience you. Think of the people you encounter every day—your family, friends, colleagues, people you interact with on social media. How would they describe you to someone who has not met you?

3. **Next, take a look at your two lists.** How many things from your first list are also on your second? Which items are missing? What would it take—people, situations, circumstances—for you to reveal the parts of you on the first list to your colleagues, your friends, your family? What conditions would you need to feel comfortable or safe stepping into your true self? Write it down.

4. **Now, ask yourself the question:** If you could do one thing to close the gap between how most people see you and who you really are, what one shift could you make? Finish the following sentence: *If you really knew me . . .*

5. **What might change** if you shared more of your first list with the world?

CHAPTER 5

TAKE INVENTORY

I am ready to . . . live what I believe.

The question: What do I believe?
The practice: Show up for your values.
The action: Align Your Beliefs with Your Behaviors.

Quick: name your top five movies.

Now, your five favorite songs.

It might have taken you a minute or two to decide which ones would make the cut, but you had a general idea. Spotify is there to remind us at the end of each year that we like K-pop or nu metal more than we'd like to admit. And we probably know exactly what we'll binge on Netflix next weekend.

Now, take a moment to think about your five most important values.

I suspect that list is a bit harder to put into words.

Our values are those beliefs that get to the core of who we are. They reflect what is sacred to us. When we're aligned with our values, they can act as a guiding force, giving us remarkable clarity about how to tackle even the hardest decisions.

But our values are rarely top of mind. Unlike your favorite films or songs, values lie dormant deep in the recesses of our souls. It often takes acute moments of misalignment to thrust our values onto center stage of our attention, forcing us to assess if and how they actively show up in our daily lives.

I got my first glimpse of how it feels to live in alignment with myself as soon as I set foot in New York City for college. There, I discovered a mecca of international blending—a beautiful collision of people from all walks of life, cultures, and countries. Leaving my suburban, middle-class, predominantly white upbringing for Manhattan was an electric experience. Having grown up brown in a sea of white, I struggled with seeing anything beautiful about myself. I felt like the ugly duckling—I was literally told that I *was* an ugly duckling. It wasn't until my move to New York that my sense of self completely flipped.

At university, I cultivated Asian friendships and community for the first time. I found myself gravitating towards fellow Asians on campus and in class, longing to embrace and integrate my Chinese roots. Somehow, these roots felt like home to me in this new place, far away from where I'd been raised. I felt a safety being with them, a kinetic sense of connection and instant acceptance born of shared understanding. I learned in college that though I'd spent years adapting to my surroundings, what I craved was to reclaim and reintegrate my culture and heritage. By seeing my racial identity through the eyes of others who appreciated it, I learned to embrace it in ways I had not been able to before. I also began to understand and explore my deepest values.

I wish I could say that I carried that college experience into my career, but when I began working in advertising, I found myself once again in a primarily white world with very few Asians around me. Life went on—I changed jobs, fell in love, got married, and began to enjoy some of the external markers of success I had long pursued. I wasn't actively pursuing the safety of assimilation, but I see now that I was inadvertently drifting away from the sense of kinship and connection to my heritage I had discovered at university.

And then, 2020.

Days after the murder of George Floyd, I was in a meeting with the partners at our agency about how to respond and show up for our BIPOC employees. Though our agency was known for innovative campaigns fighting gender inequality and racial injustice, one of our young Black strategists called out our leadership group for our silence in the wake of Floyd's death. In a powerful and unwavering company-wide email, she cracked the egg wide open, and our leadership team grappled with the call for accountability and action.

It was tense, both within myself and in the collective atmosphere of the agency. Emails flew across the company—igniting conversations that compelled everyone to self-examine and re-evaluate. It was a moment of reckoning about how each of us navigated the world, and it prompted me to take a close look at myself: Whose values drove my actions? Were they adopted or authentic to me?

I was gripped by how deeply at odds my values were with the ways I showed up in my life. While it was clear in my heart of hearts that I was ready to reclaim my heritage, I struggled to see how I could or would undo a lifetime of practiced and ingrained assimilation. How do I translate my reawakened "knowing" into my everyday choices and behaviors? As I reflected on the violence against Asian Americans and the nation-wide reckoning of white supremacy, the tension between who I am and what I do came into sharp focus.

Around this time, a colleague forwarded a link to a film called *The Color of Fear*, a documentary shot in the mid-nineties by Lee Mun Wah. The film featured men of different ethnicities sitting in conversation with each other over the course of a weekend retreat. One moment in particular stood out—an Asian man shared his memory of waiting in line at a grocery store. The cashier pointed to the white customer behind him and said, "Next!"—ignoring his existence, rendering him invisible.

As the man spoke, memories of my own history of invisibility as an Asian American came rushing forward within me, times I was lumped in with people of color while at other times assumed to be white, not of color at all. The most painful were the times of feeling erased, overlooked, or that only one facet of my identity was being engaged at the expense of the others. I know that many Asians feel this way: unseen. I'd cultivated a loudness within me; that eighth-grade choice was to become bold and insistent—to push myself out of my shyness and onto the stage, to build the muscles for discomfort *because* of that invisibility. I had used that emboldened voice to pursue my outward ambitions, goals aligned with my first mountain climb. But in this moment, I was hit with the calling for my voice to express the full force of my values. In *The Color of Fear*, the man named and validated my personal experience, and the tension of that company-wide email became impossible to suppress or ignore.

It was mid-pandemic, so our partner meeting was held over Zoom. One of our partners read an email he'd received that morning from someone outside the agency, criticizing our public-facing Black Lives Matter messages as hypocrisy since we were an "all-white leadership" group.

At that moment, something in me unzipped. I calmly pointed out that while we didn't have any Black partners, there were, in fact, two Asian partners in our group, me included; then, thanking the stars that the meeting was a videoconference, I turned off my camera as a rush of emotions overtook me. I was flooded by guilt for how much I'd rejected my own culture and heritage, assimilating into a system of white privilege since the eighth grade. And as a result of that assimilation, few people in my daily life—friends, coworkers, neighbors—perceived me as Asian. Inside I screamed, "I am Chinese, not white!" My glasses fogged up, and tears poured out. I was overcome by waves of sobs, the classic ugly cry.

Then I heard someone in the meeting ask, "What's that sound? Is someone crying? Is everything okay?"

I forgot to mute myself.

I panicked. I sat frozen, staring at the uncomfortable faces on my screen. Silence. I prayed to the universe that this wasn't really happening. But it was—and I had the choice to remain unseen or to speak up.

I took a deep breath. I turned my video back on and faced the other partners. My puffy, tearstained face stared back at me from my frame.

"No, I'm not okay," I started. Decades of silently swallowing casual indignities poured through me—quietly dismissing, explaining away, giving those with power and privilege the benefit of the doubt. Even trickier to confront were the subtle, hidden, almost invisible ways inequity plays out in day-to-day business—when privileged traits are held as standards of excellence, favoring the outgoing, dynamic, and captivating while overlooking quieter forms of intelligence and expression. My body shook from the release of decades-old injustices locked within the vault of my soul. While the pains of my personal history were certainly palpable, my values as a leader surged through me, taking command of my words. Out poured a diatribe about how it was not enough to just support our BIPOC employees. It was our responsibility to change our culture and approach to business.

I spoke of my own guilt by assimilation. I stressed that until we owned the problems at our most senior ranks, nothing real or meaningful would change. And as I spoke, I began to see the changes I needed to make as a leader and manager. It felt like an out-of-body experience. In fact, it was the ingredients of a new Life Brief showing up in real time.

It was becoming clear to me that there were narratives, old, outdated furniture in our collective conscience, in desperate need of rearranging, if not downright replacing. It was time to revise and reframe our definitions of good work, how we make it, and whom we celebrate in and around it. Personally, it was time for me to face the ways I had adopted, absorbed, and acted on values and beliefs that were not mine, but had served my survival and then my ambitions. I needed to dig into and uncover deeper truths—and use those truths to better our place of work.

My dear friend and colleague Christine Chen, another Chinese-American leader and partner in the agency, brought this into focus for me. During an all-agency meeting after the 2021 murders of six Asian women in Atlanta, she poignantly said, "We cannot see others until we see ourselves." That prompted a personal epiphany—that in order to be an effective champion of equity for others, I needed to first actively examine my own issues around race and identity.

How could I change something that I had not fully faced myself? Whose values have I been supporting or defending—mine or someone else's? In what ways had I played it safe rather than do what I knew was right? What other values lay dormant simply because I had chosen not to pursue or embody them?

With these questions driving me, I began to write furiously. Memories I didn't want to face came bubbling to the surface. A time when I explained away a senior director's offensive statement ("It was an unintentional mistake") when I should have confronted the director instead. How often do we excuse or forgive the actions of someone in a privileged position because of their intent? How rarely do we extend the same courtesy to those who are wronged?

I thought, too, of the moment when my son's face went blank when he was asked by a teacher to share his origin story—it dawned on me that in my quest to assimilate, I'd taught my children little about the richness of their heritage. I had blended and bled into the Western society I immigrated into—I lived in a white community, and I worked in a predominantly white industry. As I immersed myself in the messiness of a new Life Brief, I was hit by the hard realization of my own complicity in the problems—the times I had subjugated my own identity in order to achieve safety and success. In doing so, I had again lost my connection to a core value—my Chinese heritage.

And by accepting the premise that there was safety in assimilation, I had failed to make my corner of the world more equitable for others. It pained me to see the ways I had underserved my own BIPOC and Asian employees.

The road to equity is filled with potholes. Culture is the oxygen we breathe; it's invisible to those who rely on it. And it is easy to allow the culture of our environment—whether it's at work, in our communities, or with friends—to dictate how we behave and spend our time. I'm still reckoning with the moments I tried to calm the waters instead of demanding that we face the storm, the moments I traded my truth for acceptance, and the moments I defended the perpetrator instead of the victim.

The insights that surfaced during the creation of my new Life Brief resulted in a renewed sense of purpose in my work and leadership. When I distilled my thoughts and feelings together, I was able to identify four key themes. This is what it read:

- Comfort is a cornerstone of privilege and an enemy to change. The truth is unsettling and uncomfortable, but necessary. I'm ready to lean into it.
- I choose to be the leader who listens more, speaks less, and creates space for those who need to be heard.
- Our obsession with solutions, ideas, and innovations distracts and distances us from the core issues. True equity and lasting change come from deepening our relations with one another.
- I'm ready to focus on relations, not just solutions.

This last point became the name of my Leadership Brief: "Relations, Not Just Solutions." At the heart of this Brief was an insight I'd gained from Lee Mun Wah, the director of the documentary that had unlocked me. He said that when we focus on "innovation and solutions"—big ideas and sweeping practices—it becomes easy to distance ourselves from the discomfort of real change. Real change is learning to be in relationship with people who are different and divergent from us—we grow from the ups, downs, and bumpiness of sharing space, sharing conversation, sharing ideas with people who live and think differently.

When ideas overshadow relationships, it becomes easy to overlook or forget the potency of true communion with others. Sure, I'd worked on campaigns that addressed critical social issues, but how much meaningful time did I spend in community with those different from me? I realized I had the opportunity to create foundational change around me, in our agency, as a parent, and within my communities. But it would require deeper engagement with the messiness of my own identity—as well as those of the people around me. It would demand sitting and staying in the emotional messiness of relationships, especially when they become fraught, frustrating, and at times, infuriating.

I have been navigating the depths of relational commitment ever since—at work and at home. At work, it has meant deepening the values of an agency that prides itself on going beneath the surface to understand people. I now prioritize one-on-one weekly meetings with junior employees and employees who are members of underrepresented groups. Those meetings matter because I want to hear and learn from their experiences of working at the agency in real time. I want to get to know them as individuals and sit with them in whatever they're going through—even if it's uncomfortable.

What's become clear to me in this practice is that systems of privilege in the workplace extend far beyond recruiting, retention numbers, and even pay equity. My Brief clarified for me that the onus on those in positions of power is to create a culture that's safe for everyone to speak up and to be seen.

In our business, conversations move at lightning speed. It's difficult to get a word in edgewise if you don't feel safe speaking up around figures of authority. One day, a few months after that fateful Zoom meeting, one of our senior account directors stopped halfway through a meeting and asked, "Are there any thoughts that have been left off the table?" This question created space for everyone to pause and reflect on the conversation. It was a simple, yet significant, act of open leadership. In meetings like this one, junior employees often feel intimidated about speaking up. But in this moment of reflection, one of our Black strategists said, "It would be a big deal if we cast a Black doctor instead of a white doctor in this commercial. All the storyboards are of a white doctor."

A leader asking for and inviting her voice made it happen. This is how change begins. This is what "relations, not just solutions" means.

The team readily agreed. The account director had taken a moment to give the room space to connect and reflect before we rushed on to the next topic. By inviting the rest of the room to participate in the conversation, he made clear that every voice had value. Without that permission, our strategist would likely have left the meeting holding her idea, possibly never expressing it, because the space was not created for her voice to break through. This type of moment has many layers of impact, both within our agency and on a grander scale. It's powerful for employees to voice their ideas and see them received by the leaders of the team. Our clients were given the opportunity as a leading brand to normalize Black women in influential and respected positions.

This moment, and many others like it, emboldened me to be more vocal in the face of power when it comes to equity. I'm a practiced extrovert, a dynamic presenter, a leader who can own the room—but I'd been quiet on issues of gender and race. I had been quiet about my identity as a woman of color. I had allowed my invisibility to work for me when it was convenient. These were things that I denied in order to function, survive, and be successful in a culture that I could no longer defend.

My "Relations, Not Just Solutions" Brief was centered around showing up with a bigger voice for the people I lead to those higher up at the agency, and to everyone around me. I felt driven to use my voice, my authority, my leadership, and my influence to make meaningful and lasting change—and I needed to do it one on one, one-by-one, and on repeat.

Equity has no finish line. It's an active effort required by each person who walks into the agency whom we have the honor of employing, growing, and celebrating. As leaders, we get to demonstrate what it looks like to work in a place that is evolving consciously towards a more equitable existence.

This is how we can show up for our values, bringing them out into the open, affecting the way we view the world and our lives. Tension, when it arises—as it did on the day of my colleague's poignant all-agency email, as it did on the day I tearfully spilled my shame on Zoom—can serve as a powerful wake-up call that your values are out of alignment with your actions.

How can you bring back the balance?

The Action:
Align Your Beliefs with Your Behaviors

Identifying your beliefs is not always an easy process. It requires deep listening and reflection to invite them forward—and, as with every other aspect of the Life Brief, we never consider this exploration one-and-done.

Tune into your quiet. Find a space where you can get comfortable, relax, and reflect. As always, you should have something to write with and something to write on. Once you are settled and centered, write your thoughts about the following questions. And if more questions arise while you are writing, allow your curiosity to follow them.

In thinking about a relationship, your work, yourself, a cause, or community you care about . . .

- What does it mean to be a good _____
  (partner, child, friend, parent, employee, boss, citizen, etc.)?
- What does it mean to do good work?
- What does it mean to treat yourself right?
- What does it mean to be of service?

Now I want you to think about how to "activate your beliefs." For me, that meant opening myself up to learning. Every day, I made space to learn about embracing true equity. I read, I listened, and I took action, whether that meant finding an article about how to be antiracist or having a conversation with a colleague—and rarely did I end up doing only one thing per day.

Ask yourself, if you could activate one of your most sacred beliefs, which would it be?

What is one small, simple, immediate action I can take in service of this belief?

What is one big, audacious action I can take in service of it?

Choose something that excites and energizes you, even if it makes you nervous.

CHAPTER 6

NAME YOUR LEGACY

I am ready to . . . listen to my calling.

The question: How do I want to be remembered?

The practice: Harness the tension.

The action: Pen Your Eulogy.

Harvard professor Tom DeLong teaches that there is a friction between our "résumé values" and our "eulogy values." Résumé values drive our tangible achievements, the things we list on our CVs about who we are by way of what we've accomplished. Our eulogy values, on the other hand, offer clues to our deeper callings, how we hope to be remembered, the legacy we'd like to leave behind.

These two sets of values can coexist, creating a tension that can be harnessed to help forge new paths unique to us. But that's not always immediately clear. Just after I was promoted to strategy director and was leading my own teams and accounts, this tension manifested in a tug-of-war between my desire to hold a successful strategy career and a longing to do more with it. I loved my work at GS&P, working alongside and learning from the smartest, most imaginative, and funniest minds in our industry.

Yet I had a gnawing sense that I wanted to do work that felt more, well, *meaningful.* I yearned to do more with my skills and experience—to aim them beyond commercial outputs, to be of greater service, and to impact people in deeper and lasting ways. It was at this time that a tension emerged—one that would fuel my career decisions for decades to come.

Have you ever felt the kind of tension I'm talking about? When it feels like you could *technically* keep things the way they are and still pay the bills, squeeze in time for family and friends, and live a good enough life? Have you ever worried that underneath the familiarity of "good enough," you feel a tug towards a divergent path? Sometimes this occurs when you've finally scaled that "first mountain," only to find that it didn't bring the feeling of satisfaction or completion you'd hoped for. Other times, this can come when you are feeling a disconnect between the values that matter most to you and the day-to-day things that dominate your time. It's a kind of tension that can feel quiet but nagging or desperately urgent, depending on the severity of the misalignment.

In advertising, tensions signal opportunities to provoke engagement, stir debate, and ultimately capture attention. When it comes to an agency's creative process, tension is often where the fruit is. We look for ways to play into or provoke tension—amplifying a conflict that exists in a category or culture. Tension typically arises when the status quo grates against a desire or readiness for change. It requires reflection or active investigation to get to the source. Sometimes, you may not even realize you're wishing for something different, but next time you're feeling uneasy, resistant, or downright grumpy, take a minute to ask: What am I reacting to in this moment? What's making me feel this way? Am I going along with something even though I don't agree? Is there another path that I want to pursue instead? What is it that I really want?

Here's an example. At the height of Ben & Jerry's success with its crazy concoctions of ice cream flavors, Häagen-Dazs found itself struggling for relevance. As wild flavors and surprising combinations flooded supermarket freezer aisles, our agency team helped Häagen-Dazs take an opposing point of view—not just through marketing but with their product as well. We launched Häagen-Dazs Five, a series of rich, single-flavor ice creams made with only five ingredients. Countering more-is-more with a less-is-more point of view helped Häagen-Dazs regain relevance during a time of competitive threat.

In life, tensions offer clues to deeper truths. When we get curious about the sources of tension, we begin to answer questions like, *How is what I'm doing different from what I believe in? Where's the gap between where I stand and where I long to be?* And, *What will it take for my values to shine through?*

So how do we get more tuned into the tension? How do we explore it, unpack it, and use it to drive meaningful change?

About a decade into my advertising career, I began to feel restless. I wrestled with "this or that" thinking—either stay in a job that I was good at and paid well, or take a full leap onto a more meaningful path. I didn't think I could have it both ways.

I was carrying a story or belief that there are only two paths, a financially stable one in which I have little agency or a meaningful one in which I have lots of independence but less stability—when my heart was yearning for an alternate path.

I dug into my eulogy values, searching for a way to reconcile these seemingly opposing paths. And as I did, I began to see that perhaps there was a third way forward. Years before I introduced my colleagues to the Life Brief, I had cofounded a company called Juice with a mission to help people uncover and name their strengths and motivations—essentially, what gets them juiced. In many ways, it was a beta version of the Life Brief, a short-lived precursor that went dormant until it was reawakened a decade later.

When the agency made the call for leaders to teach something personal, a doorway reopened. It was an invitation to take my understanding and curiosity about what drives people, what motivates people, what gives them a sense of purpose and possibility—and use that to support people across the agency. That first talk I did on the Life Brief was a chance for my eulogy values to come busting through—for me to reinterpret my calling and to bring it back in a new form that braided together my résumé values with my eulogy values.

My day job and my calling wove together with parenting and leadership, born from the same *why*:

How do I unlock purpose, possibility, motivation, and drive in others?

Today, I create time for my eulogy values while showing up for the responsibilities of my résumé values. The tension between these two sets of values drives my choices and actions, weaving a rich tapestry of life experiences. And it's in this tension that we can all find fuel for our growth. My epiphany in becoming a partner of the agency was, *Wow. I get to do this human-centered work now as a leader.* And I can do the same as a parent to my four kids. I could harness my beliefs—the tools, approaches, and practices at the core of my value system—to shape and shepherd them in small and big ways. It wasn't until much later that I could see that my pursuit of and passion for human motivation is available to me in *everything* I do.

This is one of the most powerful aspects of this practice—it's not just big leaps, but also a slow unfolding. Sure, my Briefs have inspired me to make some bold moves—from literally packing up the family and moving to a new city, to walking into my boss's office and laying out a new vision for my role. But more often than not, my Life Briefs have helped me reimagine and recommit to my most significant long-standing relationships. The aim of the Life Brief isn't to prompt drastic life changes. It's designed to shift the way we see ourselves, our opportunities, and our personal agency to create what we want from what we already have, right here and now. For me, it's meant realizing the many ways I was already living in alignment with my values—and ways I could do more in each part of my life.

Look for and lean into the tensions that bubble up in your life. Don't give in to any reflexes to avoid or dismiss them. Comfort breeds complacency, while tension is a propeller of momentum. Harness your restless agitation and use it to push you forward. Follow its heat, and you'll be amazed at what you harvest.

The Action: Pen Your Eulogy

One of the exercises strategists use in research is to ask people to write a eulogy or epitaph for a brand. This helps us uncover what makes that brand special and the role it plays in people's lives. I'm always surprised by the depth of responses we receive, not to mention the poetry and poignance of people's writing.

In the Life Brief, this same exercise helps you think about how you want to be remembered, revealing clues about what matters most to you.

Imagine the celebration of your life after you are gone. What do you want to be said about you? How do you hope your friends, family, and loved ones will describe you or your impact on them? What traits and qualities do they note? What roles or experiences do you want them to highlight? What impact do you want to make as a person, partner, child, or friend?

CHAPTER 7

FACE YOUR ENEMIES

I am ready to . . . confront my monsters.

The question: What holds me back?
The practice: Name your doubts.
The action: Mine Your Limiting Beliefs.

One of the exercises strategists use to help brands get clear about who they are is to "name their enemies"—beliefs, behaviors, ideas, or ideologies that stand in the way of a brand's mission or ambition. It's energizing for marketing teams to know not only what they stand for, but also what they stand against—be it pollution, complacency, or excess. Enemies allow companies to align with their consumers through a shared belief, mission, or cause. The more clearly you define an enemy, the easier it becomes to see it and disable it.

In life, and in Life Briefs, enemies are internalized ideas and ideologies that inhibit us from realizing our deepest desires. In fact, some of your own might have already revealed themselves as you've been reading this book. Enemies show up in many forms—as resistance, self-doubt, or what I call the isms: skepticism, cynicism, realism, perfectionism. They can also take the form of social taboos, rules, or standards we adhere to without an understanding of why. Regardless of form, these internalized monsters are commonly rooted in limiting beliefs, deeply held ideas about yourself or the world that hold you hostage.

When it came to my earliest Life Briefs, I danced around the question of money—referring to it but not addressing it head-on. There was something about directly addressing it, even privately to myself, that felt taboo, dangerous, like a trap for my soul. I was defiant about not writing about it in my Life Brief—that should have been a sign that I needed to think about the role that money was playing in my life. Because if I were to be honest, it was top of mind more frequently than I dared to admit.

When I finally gathered the courage to name my personal enemies and limiting beliefs around money and finances, I saw the roots of my limitations in my extended family history. Both sides of my family had achieved great wealth and influence in China but lost everything during the Communist takeover.

My parents, like many children of means in that era, immigrated to the United States seeking a better education and a fresh start. But, once they arrived, stripped of their personal histories, my parents became just another set of Chinese immigrants. My father, who grew up with wealth, privilege, and prominence as the son of an esteemed governor and accomplished military general, struggled to adapt to this change. Though his childhood friends made names for themselves—a Harvard dean and a celebrated artist among his oldest circle of friends—my father endured layoffs, unemployment, and eventually, the misfortune of starting a real estate venture just before a recession.

He had arrived in the US armed with ambition and roaring with confidence. He generously helped countless others navigate the terrain of immigration and set up life in America. But the shame of what he perceived as his failures took its toll.

We used to return to Taiwan every December holiday, bearing suitcases stuffed with gifts from America—assorted boxes of See's Candies, shampoos, conditioners, soaps, and lotions you couldn't find in Taipei at the time. I realize in hindsight that these gifts were small symbols of abundance and achievement, showing that we had "made it" in the West. The main reason for our annual visits was to see my grandmother, the matriarch of our family and center of my father's love and loyalty. He was her only son, the pride of her life.

When my father hit financial bottom with the closure of his real estate company, his shame peaked to the point that he could no longer face his mother. He stopped accompanying us on our annual holiday trips. Though his love and loyalty never wavered, he never returned to see her again. He continued to send her money and called her without fail every Sunday morning, but he could no longer look her in the eyes. Three decades passed before her death. He never saw his mother alive again.

My childhood was colored by my father's unpredictability. His boisterous and booming joy gave way to alcohol-fueled rage, isolation, and depression. I can still feel the dread of waiting for him to come home, holding our breath, not knowing which version of Dad would walk through the door. We never knew what might set him off. Whenever there was a blowup, my dad would threaten to kill himself or the cat. We spent our childhood evenings walking on eggshells, emotionally preparing for the night's roller coaster.

While I didn't understand what weighed on him then, I do now—the pressures of raising a family, keeping the finances going, juggling the stressors that come with it. Add to this a layer of cultural expectation, lack of self-worth, and attachment to a narrow definition of success. What I did know at a very young age was that I was not going to be driven by those same markers or measures.

As I neared adulthood, my mom once impressed on me, "Marry someone who will give you financial security." The irony is that though my mother wed for financial security, my father's depression became so severe over the years that she ended up becoming our family's sole breadwinner.

This dynamic fed my earliest relationship with money; I saw how much of my parents' struggles and personal choices were financially driven. I saw the consequences of my mom's choice to marry for security. I witnessed how intertwined my dad's pride, self-worth, and esteem were with his financial success. These themes subconsciously informed my own beliefs later in life, culminating in the idea that financial success demands severe personal sacrifice. Imprinted deep within me was an either-or belief that money is a direct trade-off to personal happiness and well-being. I understood the social value of it, of course, but struggled with my internal feelings that took root as I watched my family suffer.

I didn't want my own marriage to mirror my parents'. Chip and I had already been mired in financial struggles during the early years of our relationship. Thankfully, we shared many of the same values around money—we had both been raised to value the mileage we got out of it. He'd been raised by a frugal family of bankers, and I'd grown up with my mother's incredible immigrant resourcefulness. (Cue memories of her boarding a plane after Thanksgiving with a frozen turkey carcass in a Ziploc bag tidily packed in her suitcase to make soup the next day— needless to say, I was raised to hate waste of any kind!)

But my childhood also left me with a hot mess of a relationship with money. I never realized how much my parents were struggling because appearances were so important to my dad. When he'd give me a twenty-dollar bill to pay for snacks at school, how could I think we were anything but well-to-do?

Yet, as much as our core values were aligned, Chip and I had very different comfort levels around what we spent money on and what we didn't. I witnessed how fraught and fragile our relationship became as we wrestled with the rising costs of raising a family in the Bay Area while needing to carve out more time for our kids and each other. As someone whose job it is to study behavioral trends, I knew that many marriages end as a result of financial instability. Thus, it was a friction I was intent on eliminating for our family.

Without realizing it, I had developed a limiting belief that any conversations about money would end in strife. I was so intent on not letting money become a source of tension in our marriage that it became difficult to have honest conversations about our financial goals. Money talk had become an enemy that was preventing us from aligning as a couple and a family.

Limiting beliefs can exist about anything, big or small. They can exist around school, work, parenting, success, and even *wanting* itself. "I've been taught that wanting will always lead to disappointment," said a woman in one of my Life Brief workshops. And while it took me some time to understand this, I came to realize that my limiting belief about the link between money and suffering led me to fear financial success. My resistance to declaring my desire for financial stability and even abundance held me back in practical ways—negotiating for my worth in my salary, accepting lower rates for consulting or coaching, and giving away the value of my wisdom and experience for free.

It took me many iterations of Life Briefs before I could push myself into a place of acknowledgment and self-awareness that moved me past financial self-doubt. Long before I could ever write about money or finances, I was able to say, "I want abundance." (Almost immediately after that, I got pregnant with our fourth child—a most welcome blessing, but perhaps a lesson to be a little more specific in my Life Briefs!)

I worked my way to being able to say, "I never want to experience financial anxiety again"—a hot button of stress and tension in our marriage. Later, I pushed myself to acknowledge my desire for "earned financial freedom." And then I went deeper still. "Why does it have to be 'earned'? Why do I need to include a qualifier?"

Each push in my Life Brief was followed by a new level of financial growth, many of them unanticipated. That's part of the mystery and magic of the Life Brief journey. It is often paved with serendipitous surprises.

So yes, enemies are within and all around us. But they lose their power once you can name them for what they are. Once you recognize your limiting beliefs, you can reassess your situation and reimagine it.

Some people have limiting beliefs about love—that love doesn't happen for those over a certain age, or for "people like us," or without compromising important parts of ourselves. "This or that" choices also box us in to narrow paths in life. *I must choose between wanting a career or a family* might seem a cliché example, but how many of us have internalized some version of it? Another is the belief that *we are not enough*—we aren't capable enough, mentally strong enough, secure enough, attractive enough, educated enough, wealthy enough, or worthy enough. Our limiting beliefs can also be directed at the people around us, keeping them trapped in small, predictable boxes. Other common limiting beliefs revolve around *not having enough*—we don't have enough time, connections, support, experience, access, talent.

Limiting beliefs can become enemies if we don't put them into perspective. They condition us to accept conventional parameters of success, keep us cocooned in our current circumstances, and hold us back from imagining what could be. This can leave us feeling stuck with no way out—often not realizing that it's a trap we have constructed for ourselves. We expect others to stay in familiar boxes, too—inside the lines, on the script, and within the rules.

As I've taught the Life Brief practice around the country, I've encountered people wracked by beliefs holding them back from what they truly want. Before doing her Life Brief, Regan, whom we met in chapter 3, believed that people wouldn't accept the real her, or that she wasn't interesting without the confidence she got from alcohol. Only when she quit drinking did she discover that people found her even more engaging *without* the influence of alcohol. Not only that, she *enjoyed* who she was without it. But these revelations came only when she was able to challenge the enemy that told her she wasn't enough on her own.

Another example of how limiting beliefs can hold us back comes from a public school teacher named Lauren. Lauren found herself gripped with anxiety each morning before heading to work. As she struggled with the rigid rules of the school system, politics among the teaching staff, and the chaos of overcrowded classrooms, her anxiety didn't subside during school hours. It only intensified.

By the middle of the school year, her situation had become intolerable. Lauren was an incredible teacher full of inventive approaches to teaching writing and math. She held visions of teaching kids outdoors while inviting and invigorating their own creative forces. She longed to go beyond the strict confines of a stifling and ineffective curriculum.

Lauren was surrounded by other teachers who were unsupported and exhausted, jostling for advancement while drained from the lack of resources in the overcrowded classrooms. She desperately wanted to leave, but she was the only consistent and reliable source of support for her two kids—she made up her mind to shoulder the anxiety she experienced at work in return for the stability of the paycheck. "Isn't this what responsible parenting is all about?" Lauren asked. She had not yet realized this was a limiting belief—that she had to remain tethered to this anxiety-inducing role to support her family.

The misalignment ate away at her self-confidence. As the year progressed, she woke up each morning with paralyzing dread about what lay ahead.

One day, the principal announced that each teacher would take turns teaching to the entire grade while other teachers observed—implementing a system of peer critique among a faculty already rife with politics and burnout. The news broke Lauren. How could she teach a curriculum she didn't believe in while being evaluated by her peers? She could no longer continue this cycle of angst that left her too emotionally drained to engage in the other important parts of her life. But how could she leave when she had her children to think of?

Lauren pulled out her notebook, pouring out the frustrations she had with her job and financial situation. Through the act of writing, she discovered her limiting belief, a "this or that" choice that held her hostage in a pattern of anxiety and exhaustion:

I have to choose between keeping this job to support my children or finding a role that truly fulfills me.

Recognizing the limits of this belief was a final straw—she turned her focus to what *would* fulfill her. She set aside her anxiety and tuned in to her curiosity in earnest. She created space to reflect on and dig into deeper questions about her work:

- What does it mean to do good work?
- What fills me and lights me up about my work?
- What am I devoted to?
- What do I want to bring to my work that I'm not bringing today?
- What do I want for my work to bring me?

After much reflection and several Brain Dumps later, Lauren sat down and wrote a Life Brief around what she needed to become the thriving and inspired teacher she knew she was.

- The freedom to teach with imagination, experimenting with inventive approaches to fulfill my students' needs.
- The freedom to see my students for who they are, not just their rank in class or their test scores.
- The freedom to bring nature and creativity into my classroom with outdoor teaching and role-playing to enhance my students' imagination.

- The freedom to create a schedule that works for my
  family and me, while earning what we need to thrive.

She called her Life Brief "Freedom to Educate." Soon after, Lauren left her job as a middle school teacher and turned her focus to what she truly desired in her role as an educator. Today, Lauren leads sold-out camps and after-school classes that she designed based on her own pedagogy. She has a flexible schedule that allows her to blend her teaching with parenting and her own creative writing projects. Not only is her income higher, Lauren feels more fulfilled and is reaching more students than she would have if she had stayed on her original path.

Lauren crossed a difficult gauntlet when she wrote her Life Brief. She had to face the fears she had about being able to support her family and reconcile them with the exhaustion she felt doing her job. But when she finally identified the limiting belief that trapped her in place, Lauren was able to see a path that allowed her to have both the security and the fulfillment she craved.

The process of naming our big ideas, then figuring out the ways to make them actionable, is what we do in advertising. It's not about declaring that we want to be rich; it's about specifying the things that matter to us, the questions that grip us, and the stories clouding our perception of what's possible. We must face down the enemies that tell us we cannot escape restriction, sacrifice, or complacency.

Our limiting beliefs can be inherited from our families, our experiences, cultural norms, or social expectations. Understanding what holds us back from committing to what we want allows us to reassess where those enemies lie within us. We can openly acknowledge how deep our limiting beliefs penetrate and how far back their origins are.

Limiting beliefs can be hard to get rid of, especially because they are so deeply embedded inside of us. But these feelings don't have to consume us. We can face our internal enemies and reimagine them. We can steer our attention towards what lights us up and open new paths for pursuing what we desire.

Today, I have learned to ignore the belief that talking about and taking charge of money will only lead to suffering. Not only has this enabled my family to manage our finances more openly but it has also allowed us to expand our conversations about our values. Thanks to my ability to state my desire for abundance, I have shifted my attention—and my ideas about wealth. Today, my driving questions about money are *What is enough? What do we need for the life we want?* and *What kind of wealth matters most to me?*

In order to defeat our enemies, we must first acknowledge and understand them. Acknowledging them is the first step to confronting them. Acknowledgment comes in the form of naming them and writing them down—only then can we change our story.

The Action: Mine Your Limiting Beliefs

For each of the four areas in your life—relationships, work, self, and community or cause—think about moments of doubt or resistance you have experienced either in the recent past or right now, in this very moment. These thoughts often begin with *I can't, I'm not, It isn't, They don't,* or something similar. Some examples:

- They won't find the real me interesting.
- I can't provide for my family doing the type of job I really want.
- A person like me doesn't get to choose what I want to do.
- I'm not qualified to do anything else, so I have to accept where I am.
- I'm not _____ enough to _____.

Self-inquiry master Byron Katie uses three simple questions to test the validity of long-held, limiting beliefs. As you list each of yours, ask yourself, *Is this belief true? What evidence do I have that it is true? Who would I be or how would my life be different without this belief?*

I'm going to be honest: I have a hard time asking people to write in the negative, even as part of an exercise! But the reality is there are probably some limiting beliefs lurking underneath your awareness. Let's unearth them so that we can get rid of them.

RELATIONSHIPS

- I can't _____
  _____
- I'm not _____
  _____
- I don't _____
  _____
- They won't _____
  _____

WORK

- I can't _____
  _____
- I'm not _____
  _____
- I don't _____
  _____
- They won't _____
  _____

SELF

- I can't _____
  _____

- I'm not _____
  _____

- I don't _____
  _____

- They won't _____
  _____

COMMUNITY OR CAUSE

- I can't _____
  _____

- I'm not _____
  _____

- I don't _____
  _____

- They won't _____
  _____

Now review your list and think critically of each line: *Where did this belief come from? What proof do I have that this is true? In what ways would I show up differently if I let go of this belief?*

CHAPTER 8

REFRAME YOUR STORY

I am ready to . . . change my perspective.

The **question:** How can I change my story?

The **practice:** Reframe your situation.

The **action:** It's Not X, It's Y.

Now that you've unearthed your limiting beliefs and the enemies holding you in place, what can you do with them? Is awareness enough to make them magically disappear? How do you use this knowledge to break through the boundaries or barriers they've created in your life?

By reframing your perspective.

In many ways, the Life Brief is an art in perspective—seeing twists in the familiar, inventing unexpected solutions to old problems, challenging "what is" with "what if." This practice is about finding the joy in problem-solving—often this perspective shift is enough to enliven us where before we felt stuck, to create motion where there wasn't any.

Advertising's aim is to change perceptions and behaviors. It's the strategist's job to help people see and engage with brands in new ways.

Apple isn't just any computer or phone, it's a symbol of creativity and originality. Airbnb doesn't just offer a place to stay, it's an experience in belonging. Mastercard isn't just a credit card, it's your ticket to creating priceless memories.

Cheetos is one of GS&P's beloved client brands. The snack can also be a parent's nightmare: think orange fingerprints on the upholstery, orange dust in the car. But what we found in our research is that people who love to eat Cheetos happen to be people who also love to break rules. They're playful practical jokers with great senses of humor. They're more likely to pull pranks and skip out on school or work. This discovery inspired our agency team, in partnership with our clients, to reframe Cheetos from a finger-staining snack to a symbol of mischief—a brand that's fun, playful, and willing to poke fun at itself—and at anyone who takes life too seriously. Cheetos gives people permission to get messy, play, and rediscover their inner juvenile. We identified the tension around the snack's messiness and reframed it in a way that allowed a creative strength to emerge.

In the previous chapter, we did the hard work of speaking the unspeakable, identifying the limiting beliefs holding us back, and naming our enemies. Now we're going to approach those beliefs from a new angle. It is time to reframe your perspective, see your situation in a new light, and identify alternate possibilities and paths forward.

In teaching the Life Brief, I have met people held in suspension by a limiting belief. Once they learned to reimagine those beliefs, however, they were astonished by the opportunities that opened up. Kelly is an example of this. She had long been struggling in her marriage—the kind of suffering that isn't apparent to outsiders but inwardly feels like death by a thousand paper cuts.

Though he publicly professed to be his wife's number one fan, Kelly's husband demanded center stage in the confines of their family life. In subtle and not-so-subtle ways, he made everything about him, dominating conversations, swaying household decisions, and controlling their finances with an iron fist. His demands were frequent and intense, and even as Kelly made attempts to meet them, none of her expressed needs were being met. As a business leader, entrepreneur, and outspoken champion of gender equity, Kelly was heralded as an industry change-maker. Yet she felt suffocated and trapped in her relationship. Her internal experience didn't align with her values around partnership.

Kelly soldiered on, committed to keeping her family whole. This is not uncommon. We're trained as a society to look out for major crimes as markers for ending a relationship: cheating, gambling, physical abuse. But in many relationships, there's nothing singular, blatant, or obvious that screams, *Time's up!* Many relationships bleed out over time through a series of small yet cumulative misdemeanors.

The first questions to ask when evaluating relationships, whether they be with friends, family, or lovers, are, "Am I safe in this relationship? Am I being hurt in any way—physically, mentally, emotionally, or sexually?" If you feel unsafe, frightened, or abused in any way, then get out. No relationship is worth the cost of your health or safety.

If safety isn't a concern, the next layer of questions are, "Am I growing from this relationship? Am I learning? Am I still being stretched in healthy ways? Do I feel agitated or uncomfortable because I'm growing and evolving, or is this hard because it's draining or diminishing me?"

The answers to these questions were hard for Kelly to see. She was struggling to maintain a positive front for her kids, for their friends, and their community. It was difficult for her to imagine disrupting the identities and lives they had built together.

Often, the first response to, *What do I want?* is an answer for what we think we *should* want. With that in mind, return to your Daily Brain Dumps and the Let Your Pen Lead exercises—or any other time you've asked yourself, *What do I really want?*

How often did you answer that question with someone else's desires instead of your own?

Sometimes, in order to protect the people around us, we sacrifice pieces of ourselves. For Kelly, that was very much the case. Her priority was showing up for her kids, and keeping her marriage intact seemed like a critical part of holding things together. She was also battling a limiting belief that divorce equated to failure. *Who am I without this marriage?* So much of her identity was connected to being a woman in a committed marriage with two wonderful kids—the uncertainty of who she would become without her marriage kept her trapped. As a result, her first take on her Life Brief was a continuation of her effort to keep things together—to show up better in a bad relationship.

Kelly knew she was, in many ways, suffering, yet she wanted to give the relationship another chance. She decided that she wanted to become her husband's "Number One Fan," the same way he rallied around her publicly and socially. That became the handle of her first Life Brief. She genuinely wanted to give their relationship another chance—even if that meant changing, bending, and sacrificing more of *herself* to make the relationship work. They'd been to marriage counseling, and Kelly was committed to self-betterment. She found that in all other aspects of her life, her willingness to go the extra mile was working—in all other areas except in her marriage. Still, she thought, *If only I were more forgiving or more easygoing, if only I were stronger, if only I weren't so sensitive—things would be different.* She doubled down on what, deep down inside, she knew might be a bad decision because she felt like she'd invested too much to do otherwise.

But the hum inside her never quieted. It continued to grip and gnaw at her, despite her shifts in attitude and actions. Becoming her husband's biggest fan didn't change the way she really felt about him, and it didn't change his behavior towards her.

It got to the point where whenever Kelly thought about her "Number One Fan" handle, she would cringe. That visceral response was a clear sign that she needed to revisit her Life Brief.

Even though she was scared about what it might reveal, Kelly forced herself to sit down and write another iteration of her Life Brief—this time, confronting her limiting beliefs about what it means to end a marriage.

Often our limiting beliefs about relationships existed long before we met our significant others—we looked to the adults in our lives as models to emulate or avoid. We breathe in ideas about love and romance from movies, songs, and TV—and powerful stories begin to form when we're much too young to realize what's going on. When we learn to step back from our current perspective and ask, "Is this belief really mine?" we create space to tell different stories about what we actually need and deserve.

When Kelly opened herself up to this perspective shift, she had a "lightning rod moment," where she realized that she needed to completely reframe the way she saw her relationship and the role it played in her life. *Wait a second*, she thought to herself as she wrote. *Why do I keep writing divorce off as failure? It doesn't have to be an ending. What if it's a new adventure and my new beginning?*

That moment was the beginning of a big mental shift for Kelly. Instead of focusing on the failure of what wasn't, she would choose the life she wanted to create for herself. Once she flipped this limiting belief, her pain was replaced by a buzzing sense of possibility for what *could be*. What could she author for her own life without the heaviness of the marriage she was in?

In walking this new path, Kelly no longer felt envious or sad when she saw happily married couples; she instead felt gratified she'd reimagined a life where "everything was intentional and reciprocal." This led her to a new sense of self, freedom, and purpose that rippled through other parts of her life. She saw how much suffering her people-pleasing persona had caused her. She had been attached to that perfect family image she'd striven to uphold. But that "shiny" image as the ideal family woman wasn't worth the pain that came with it. Kelly had feared a fall from grace if this image was shattered, but once she left that limiting belief behind, she felt freer and more capable of creating the life of peace and personal success she longed to have.

By reimagining our limiting beliefs, we can move past self-reproach and free ourselves to go for what we want in life.

The Action: It's Not X, It's Y

A valuable reframing exercise used by strategists is called It's Not X, It's Y. Here's how it works. Take one limiting belief and write as many "reframes" as you can think of over five minutes. You can set a timer to help you track time.

Because some limiting beliefs are deeply tattooed into our psyches, they can feel impossible to reimagine. Give it a try anyway. Again, this is a practice. Not only will it get easier the more you do it but you'll also get more out of it.

KELLY'S LIMITING BELIEF:

I can't end my marriage without ruining the life I worked so hard to build.

KELLY'S REFRAME:

- Divorce is not failure, it's successfully letting go of a toxic situation.
- Divorce does not diminish me, it brings me back to my fullest self.

- Divorce is not an ending, it's the beginning of a new adventure.

I went through a similar process of reframing with my Brief about my relationship with money.

BONNIE'S LIMITING BELIEF:

Wanting financial abundance will only result in heartache and pain.

BONNIE'S REFRAME:

- Money is not a measure of self-worth, it's a means to self-reliance.
- Demanding my full worth is not selfish, it's self-respecting.
- True wealth is not financial, it lies in freedom of choice and personal agency.

Now you try. On the next page, pick a belief that you want to challenge and examine it from all angles.

THE LIFE BRIEF

MY LIMITING BELIEF:

_____

_____

MY REFRAME:

_____

_____

_____

_____

_____

_____

_____

_____

CHAPTER 9

LISTEN TO YOUR FANS

I am ready to . . . hear real feedback about who I am.

The question: What role do I play?

The practice: Know your magic.

The action: Interview Your Fans.

In my line of work, I've encountered clients who pay too much attention to naysayers or negative reviews, just as many of us do in our everyday lives. Constructive criticism is useful for tactical improvement and refinement, so we shouldn't ignore it completely. But when it comes to understanding a brand's potential, we encourage clients to ignore the naysayers and instead focus on feedback from their fans—people who love what they do, who are in their corner and invested in their success—because it means something to them.

The perspective and objectivity we can gain from others is the reason why companies hire agencies in the first place. Agencies aren't in the weeds of the day-to-day problems that come with running a business—we can bring clients back to a big-picture view when they are struggling to see the forest for the trees.

That's why in developing creative briefs, we ask incisive, impartial questions like, *What's special or standout about this brand compared to its competitors? What do its biggest, most loyal fans love about it?* An agency looks at a company through fresh eyes and, in doing so, inspires its clients to do the same, seeing what energized them in the first place.

This principle can be applied to our personal potential as well. Hearing from your fans can remind you of all the wonderful things you put into the world. You may be surprised by what people observe about you when they experience you at your peak. Listening to your fans allows you to harness their perspectives to highlight the things you might be missing or dismissing because you're lost in the weeds of your worries.

The lowest points in my career have been the moments when I lost myself to comparison.

Don't get me wrong. I'm a powerful presenter and persuasive presence, but I'm not a lone-wolf, "ta-da landing," smartest person in the room strategist. And because my way didn't match the mold of my predecessors, there were times that I struggled with feeling like an imposter.

As a partner of the agency, one of my primary responsibilities is to pitch for new clients. New business pitches are high-stakes, high-pressure, speed-driven dogfights against a handful of other best-in-class creative agencies. One particularly challenging pitch was for an emerging tech company. The client's problem was fascinating yet tangled, and its products were technologically complex. It was a category I was eager to master, but the speed and intensity of the pitch required more study and interrogation than I could muster. Our pitch team was stacked with competing voices. The pressure was palpable, and the timing couldn't have been worse. I was parenting four kids in the middle of a pandemic. We were navigating the turbulent waters of adolescent angst. As soon as I clicked out of my back-to-back Zoom meetings, I flew into parent mode, often late into the night. I had no space to step back to gain perspective and was struggling to see a clear strategic path through the assignment.

The pressure of this particular pitch hit me hard. I woke up each morning feeling exponentially more anxious than the morning before, falling further behind by the day. As my anxiety grew, so did my insecurity. *Can everyone see that I don't have a confident grasp of this? What kind of leader am I if I can't model the smarts expected of a masterful strategist?* My thoughts raced to ridiculous places, as they tend to do when self-doubt is triggered. I even convinced myself that I was no longer equipped to lead strategy, and I started to seriously question my role in leading the agency. I was caught up in a loop of self-doubt.

Luckily, or unluckily I suppose, this wasn't my first spinout. And I have developed a secret weapon for how to handle bouts of negative thinking and self-doubt. I reached out to my fans—because listening to the people who know and care about you is one way to sort through the clutter of your mess. Your fans are people who can see you from a healthy distance. They aren't in the trenches of your gripping issues or limiting beliefs. They're invested in your growth and able to provide you much-needed perspective.

I reached out to colleagues who have seen me in action and observed me objectively in different situations. One was Lester, a fellow partner and dear longtime friend—we'd grown up at the agency together, witnessed and weathered major life changes alongside each other. I asked Derek, our agency president. Another was a direct report whom I think of as quiet but mighty. And a fourth was a former employee whom I fondly look to as someone obsessed with all things weird—constantly introducing me to wild ideas, new trends, and strange takes on the familiar.

I deliberately reached out to people with different views of my work with the intention of gaining perspective and clarity. I asked each of them a list of questions to get down to the heart of what I needed to understand about myself.

What makes me, me?

What's my superpower as a strategist?

What do I do as a leader that helps you or others thrive?

What role am I playing when you experience me at my peak aliveness?

These questions are powerful because they focus us on who we are at our best—at our peak—so that we can find our way back during moments of insecurity or confusion. They help to nudge us back to our aliveness when our lights dim. The answers I got back were boldly honest with threads of consistency. I invited those around me to tell me what they saw in me, and their responses were confirming and buoying.

One of my fans said, "Your superpower, and it really is a superpower, is that you get the best out of others. You create the space for people to be the best that they can be. That doesn't come from giving them the 'answers.'" Another shared, "You see people, not employees. You tell people the truth about where they are and where they stand. And you do it in service of growth and fairness." And a third said, "You listen deeply and identify the one thing that is most impactful, then hold it up so everyone can build from that place." Lester, who has journeyed with me through work and friendship, observed that I seem to be most alive when helping other people come to life—that I present and re-present their ideas in ways that give them credit and credibility with clients.

Their insights both grounded and energized me. They made me realize that the intensity of the pitch had clouded my understanding of the real role I play. Instead of taking the bird's-eye view—listening deeply for the standout insights and ideas—I had leapt into the trenches, digging alongside the core team. Instead of working to create the space and conditions for the team to do their best thinking, I was adding to the intensity. The feedback from my fans spurred me to pull back, clear my head, and support our strategy leads as a sounding board—what they really needed from me all along.

I had been so plagued by thoughts of inadequacy that I'd considered leaving my job, losing sight of the real role I play for my teams and the agency. Inviting feedback from people who have witnessed me at my best helped me recognize that my doubts were stories of my own making, not reality. I was able to step back from my fears and regain perspective. But I couldn't have done it alone—the tornado of my mind was too overpowering. In order to clear out the self-punishing noise and refocus on my strengths, I needed to hear from voices I trusted, voices I valued more than the one that was telling me that I was failing.

Before you start sending out your requests for feedback, it's important to note that not all feedback is created equal. This exercise is specifically aimed at collecting feedback from people who genuinely know and respect you, but it stops short of being an open call for any kind of outside advice, opinion, or influence. Fan feedback is not meant to invite compliments or criticism from acquaintances, followers, or friends of friends. The permissiveness that comes with online anonymity and social media platforms allows for judges and critics with zero understanding of who you are to weigh in on your life.

That's why we ask a specific and limited set of questions of people we have interacted with closely enough for us to trust the information they give. By asking the series of questions from this chapter's exercise, we steer away from loose opinions or generic "advice" and instead focus on questions designed to shine light on our highest selves reflected in other people's experiences of us.

"Advice" is often what traps us in gripping tribulations in the first place. Collecting other people's opinions, like, *Should I leave my partner?* or, *What am I doing wrong in my life?* detaches us from our own internal voice. Interviewing your fans is not about seeking tactical advice; it's a quest to uncover what makes you most alive. There's a difference between asking, *What do you think I should do?* or, *Should I quit my job?* versus, *What are the traits that make me,* me? *When do I seem most invigorated and alive?*

What would happen if, instead of asking these people *who you should be* or *what you should do*, you asked them about *what they see and experience in you*?

I've encountered many people whose view of themselves has been altered after interviewing their fans. A woman in one of my workshops, named Diane, carried around the narrative that she was a negative person. She was convinced that because her skepticism and rigorous questioning about people and situations were often met with silence from others, that people found her negative and judgmental. This story about herself was rooted deeply in her psyche.

I asked her why, exactly, she felt that the outside world viewed her as a negative person. Had someone told her that she was negative? This prompted her to interview her fans. When she asked her loved ones the questions from the exercise, she was amazed to find that no one saw her as negative. In fact, what came through was that people experience her as a bright light in their lives; people relish her ability to notice things others miss or overlook. They see that her curiosity and rigor help her and the people around her avoid pitfalls and seize new opportunities. What she misread as negative was in reality welcomed and cherished.

Many of us face a similar issue. We can be overly critical or self-punishing. Interviewing your fans allows you to clear away the noise and see yourself through a new lens.

The Action: Interview Your Fans

Identify at least three people from different corners and stages of your life to interview. They can be colleagues, friends, or family, but try to have a bit of range. Invite people who are new to observing you as well as those who have been in your life for a long time, through thick and thin. Ask people who you report to and people who report to you, people you spend a lot of time with, and people whom you see less frequently.

Ideally, they see you from different angles, yet share a deep investment and support in your growth.

Ask them the following questions. Remember, these questions are designed to illuminate who we are when we're most alive. This is not a 360 degree performance review. That's the opposite of what these questions are designed to do. That's why we stick to these specific questions.

- What qualities or traits make me, me?
- What (situations, people, or things) energizes me?
- What (situations, people, or things) drains me?
- When I'm at my best, what role do I play?
- What is my superpower?

It's fascinating how much insight other people can bring to these questions. That's why I pair people up and have them interview each other in my retreats. When we invite other people into this process of deep discovery, we often see things we couldn't have seen on our own.

If your fans are willing to do so, consider going through the list together and then discussing what comes up. Ask your fans to take note of things like shifts in your body language or your tone of voice as you listen to their answers. What do they tell you?

You can also take note of these reactions yourself: don't just read the words, observe what they bring up for you.

CHAPTER 10

LEAN INTO AGITATION

I am ready to . . . face the questions I've been running from.

The question: What am I avoiding?

The practice: Ask provoking questions.

The action: Name Your Gripping Issue.

---

*W*hen *you deny what you really want, what are you protecting?*
I love this question because it instantly provokes the kind of tension that we can use. Strategists use provocations to agitate towards deeper truths. Our job is to facilitate spaces where clients can bravely confront contradictions or misalignment in service of honesty and transparency. Provocations are rarely comfortable, but they are usually effective for cutting through messiness or bullshit.

Provocations can appear when you least expect them. That's what happened to me at 7:30 a.m. one morning, when my husband asked in the middle of an argument . . .

"Are you still madly in love with me?"

I was chewing a piece of toast while packing for an overnight work trip, trying hard not to accidentally pack our youngest, who had settled herself in the middle of the pile of clean laundry on our bed.

I stopped chewing mid-bite. This was not the question I was expecting after seventeen years together, four kids, and too many hairy life transitions to count. Especially not in the middle of the kind of standard, inconsequential, born-out-of-nothing argument I had come to accept as part and parcel of a long-term relationship. His question startled me as surely as if I'd been doused with a bucket of ice water.

"Excuse me?" I blurted, incredulous. "Madly in love? What are we, teenagers?"

The truth was, it was such an earnest question that I had no good response. I panicked. Then I deflected.

"I'm late," I said, not meeting his eyes. "Let's talk later."

I went back to throwing things randomly into my suitcase. The question was unbearable. So was the answer.

No. I'm not madly in love. Not anymore.

When I thought about it, I felt like a voyeur to my own marriage. I didn't believe that mad love was possible after four kids and almost two decades of marriage. How did I—a person whose entire career as a strategist had been dedicated to a kind of universal empathy—end up feeling so distant, so resentful, so . . . stuck? Was it because I'd stopped asking necessary questions, or that I'd settled into simply believing that the monotonous routine of our love life was normal and to be expected, not something to be fought against?

Is mad love possible?

Yes, it's a common secret that many of us don't feel madly in love in our long-term relationships, but once this question entered my mind, I couldn't escape it. It gripped me and would not let go. Gripping questions are those that dominate our attention—questions we can't stop thinking about until we've found an answer for them. They seep into your consciousness, take hold, and continue to nag in your mind. The Life Brief invites us, if we truly want it, to get to the core of truth behind those burning questions.

At the time when Chip asked the question, we had just entered another period of radical change. My agency had promoted me to partner, but it had required relocating my family, which turned our lives upside down. It felt like we'd turned the page on a golden chapter of our lives, leaving a home and community we'd all adored (a house that, as I'll share later, we found as a direct result of our very first Life Brief). The move also took me back into the office five days a week, whereas I had previously been working remotely from home.

Transitions can stir up the pots of our lives, exposing where we're most vulnerable. I became the full-time at-the-office parent; Chip became the always-on stay-at-home parent, whereas before, we had carved out a blend of roles and responsibilities where I could tackle an emergency, do a pickup, take one of the kids to the doctor. In all the dividing and conquering, as so many families find themselves doing, we drifted away from each other emotionally.

When he asked me that startling question, I backpedaled; I bought time. I tried to talk my way out of the situation. But the question stuck with me, as did my avoidance of it. I couldn't escape the fact that I knew I was deflecting. The next day, I flew to Boston for an important new business pitch. But on the six-hour flight back, with no more deadlines, no more distractions to divert my attention, my mind was called back to my problem at home.

Two questions came up for me as I stared out of the window of the airplane. One, *Do I want mad love?* And if so, *Do I want it with Chip?*

Both were genuinely scary questions, and I had to sit honestly with them. To the first question, my answer was visceral and immediate. I could not imagine living the rest of my life without experiencing the exhilaration of mad love again. *What kind of life would that be?* I asked myself. *Maybe love isn't the same now as the head-over-heels love I felt at seventeen. But with 100 percent certainty, I want to feel the fire of desire for someone, and I want to be desired in that same way. Hell yes, I want mad love!*

But then came the harder question. *Do I want mad love with Chip?* This was the one I had to sit with. As good questions tend to do, this question bred more questions, each gripping me and taking me deeper within myself: *Am I still attracted to this man that I fell in love with almost two decades ago? What do I cherish about him? What do I cherish about me when I'm with him? Do I believe mad love is even possible with him?*

I pulled out my notebook and started a new Life Brief while in the air that day. I scrubbed everything else from my mind, opened a new page, and wrote, "I'm ready to fall madly in love with my husband again."

But here's the thing.

When I wrote those words, I didn't actually believe it was possible.

I wrote it down anyway. And as I began to draft my Brief, I had a series of realizations.

Despite the natural challenges that have arisen in a relationship nearing its third decade, I've always thought of Chip as my dream guy. My mind still drifts back to the moment I first saw him in that crowded meeting room—I still feel wowed by his vulnerability and open-heartedness, his quiet strength, dedication to betterment, and lack of ego. And I still feel deep attraction to him.

It's not hard to find him attractive. He's a good-looking guy—one of those men who gets better with age. But the real charm lies in how oblivious he is about it! His friends joke about going to concerts with him during their college days. A circle of women would naturally gravitate around him—and Chip would be completely unaware, lost in the music he loves so much.

What was getting in the way of mad love wasn't a lack of attraction—it was that our situation had changed and disrupted our deliberate way of being with one another. We had followed our first Brief to "Take Our Time" to a new state and a new state of mind, and it had been life-restoring.

But we now needed a new Brief to navigate the emergence of a new set of circumstances.

Sometimes, while away for a work trip, I would marinate in my love for Chip in my mind. I'd start concocting ways we could steal a moment to ourselves, plan a getaway—take advantage of an upcoming talk to explore a new city—and I'd rush in the front door ready to connect and share my ideas. But instead of the rom-com embrace I'd conjured before the plane touched down, I'd find Chip boiling a pot of pasta on the stove, kids running to share their latest news, the dog running circles around me, hoping for a walk. Or, if I'd catch him alone, he might be in full-on execution mode—ready to negotiate next week's schedules and tackle overdue decisions.

What happens when you walk in the door anticipating connection and get hit with logistics? Instant deflation.

Other times it would be me throwing buckets of ice water on *his* plans. Chip and I love to geek out on ideas together, but we brainstorm differently. As a strategist, my mind tends to shift rapidly between blue sky ideas and activation. Chip prefers to linger in the dream state, taking his time molding the clay. I can really be a cold shower on his fun when I quickly filter and eject his ideas before they've had time to gel.

In short, we're both human, and we both crave connection. But the other demands on our attention had led us to a pattern in which we rarely craved connection at the same time. I'd go so far as to say connection had started to feel damn near impossible amidst the crush of everyday life.

If we didn't even have time for basic connection, how would we ever make space for mad love?

Yes, I do want mad love, and yes, I want it with Chip.

Yet sadly, no, I did not believe it was possible.

And there began my Marriage Brief, despite my disbelief. This is a critical lesson in the Life Brief: you might not be able to *see* the how; you might not be able to *believe* the how, but the real question is, *Do you want it?*

This can be terrifying for those of us who fear these questions in the first place. We may encounter doubts like, *If I say what I want, but don't believe it's possible, am I setting myself up for heartache and disappointment?* This is where courage comes in. The Life Brief is about living creatively and living courageously. It takes courage to admit that you want something, even, and especially, when you cannot see its possibility. The courage comes from simply admitting, "*This* is what I want." Daring to write it down and to sharpen it, to drill into exactly what you want with such honesty that you feel yourself shaking a bit from facing your fears. Courage is not the same as confidence. Courage means to speak and act from a place of heart, even when you lack confidence. It's acting despite our fears, despite our limiting beliefs.

I didn't believe it could be possible, yet I wrote a Life Brief for the relationship I envisioned anyway. My Marriage Brief included being co-creators in life. In addition to mad love, I wanted us to support each other and hold each other in grace, in calm, in creativity. My handle for it was "Mad Love," and I said this phrase to myself anytime I needed a reminder about what matters most to me in our relationship. What I've found time and again with the Life Brief is that when what you want is sticky in your mind, you start to see every interaction and every choice through a new lens. (That's why in part 2 of the book, we'll explore how naming your Briefs can be a powerful tool for helping your Life Brief stick.)

When I arrived home after writing my Marriage Brief, everything was the same as it ever was. Though I had shifted, our situation had not. We had another explosive fight a week later during our annual family farm camp vacation. What I had hoped would be an idyllic week for rekindling Mad Love, peaked with a public blowup. Months of pent-up anger vented. Looking back, I can now see the wall of untended needs and unspoken truths standing between our marriage and my Mad Love Brief. Unbeknownst to me in that moment, this blowout argument was the sledgehammer we needed to take down our version of the Berlin Wall.

Of course, I thought about our first Life Brief. The very first sentence in that original Brief was centered on time—spending more time with Chip, our family, and with myself. But as often happens, our move and transition started chipping away at that time all over again. And as Chip and I threw ourselves headfirst into our different roles and responsibilities, we started to slip into separate lives again, as couples sometimes do.

At its ugliest, our argument turned towards separation . . . until Chip initiated a truce in the form of a simple hug. That physical embrace softened our stubborn stances and they gave way to tenderness and transparency. I admitted that I had been relishing the attention of another man, someone I had met on one of my work trips. And while I had no real interest in this man, his interest in me sparked an aliveness that I had been missing in our marriage. That admission unlocked the gates to real talk about other needs and neglects in our relationship. During that argument, we cracked open everything standing in the way of our ability to care for and empathize with each other—the calcified and unspoken truths standing between us and our path to mad love.

We came home from vacation emotionally spent, yet changed. One morning, during the motions of our daily routine, Chip handed me a deliciously crafted thermos of coffee on my rush out the door to my morning commute. Typically, I'd say goodbye to the kids, get in the car, and start another day. Sometimes I was already mid–work call by the time I entered the kitchen. But after writing the Mad Love Brief, shattering the silence, and opening up about our long-suppressed needs, I spontaneously leaned in and gave him a kiss. He was taken aback, clearly not expecting it. Even our kids in the kitchen paused and took note of this abnormal act of appreciation. Yet, that was it. That was the tiny catalyst on my end that we needed to kickstart us in a new direction.

In the car with my thermos of coffee, I thought, *That was lovely . . . so simple and gratifying. Why am I not doing that every morning?* And, simultaneously, a switch went off in him when I kissed and acknowledged him in that small yet significant way. I did it again the next day and again the day after that. A few nights later, while working in bed, he leaned in closer to me. And later that week, he grabbed my hand at the grocery store, another small yet unfamiliar act of intimacy.

That morning kiss served as active permission and an invitation for more. I wouldn't have thought to do it without wrestling it down and committing to it in my Mad Love Brief. Without the intentionality of the Brief at the forefront of my mind, we would have continued to stay in our own swim lanes, the distance between us growing. And though I didn't think it was possible for us to get back to the place of Mad Love, I had written it anyway because it was something that my soul craved.

Our anniversary came three weeks later. We made plans to revisit our wedding site and renew our vows. It was a ritual that we had started early on in our marriage but dropped once the busyness of four kids came into the mix. It had been a long time since we'd taken that trip just the two of us. But in the three weeks leading up to it, starting with that small, yet significant, kiss in the kitchen, we were able to reconnect and rekindle the flames of our affection. We spent three nights together out in the woods, minutes from where we were married. We watched movies and played games. We lingered over food and wine. We swam and napped at the beach. These were little things we used to enjoy but had abandoned in the busyness of our everyday routines. Yet, on this trip, we had all the time in the world.

I woke on the third morning thinking to myself, *Wait, what is this feeling? Could it be mad love?*

After I shared my Brief with Chip, he said, "Well, I guess this is the lesson. Mad love is always available to us should we want it."

This was an epiphany. Mad love is always here for our choosing, as long as we create the conditions for it to happen. We have to prioritize it, actively make space for it, and yes, ask for help when we need it. But it is always attainable, if we want it.

Now "mad love" has become shorthand, our code words. When he says, "mad love," I hear it as a reminder of our promise to each other. He's asking me, *Do you still want this? Do you still want me?* And my answer continues to be yes. That Life Brief reignited a new chapter for us, saving our marriage for the second time.

"Are you still madly in love with me?" was Chip's provocation about our relationship. The grip and agitation of his question forced me to confront my true feelings and inner conflicts so that we could break through pretense, and return to honesty and real intimacy.

It's easy for the monotonous routines of our daily lives to drown out what's most important to us, but leaning into the agitation of what grips us can unlock and invite re-engagement with what we truly desire. The answers we seek lie in the questions we tend to avoid. These gripping questions allow us to cut through our mess by fearlessly asking what needs to be asked and courageously creating the space for our bravest answers to emerge.

For many of us, our natural reflex when it comes to these uncomfortable, even unbearable, questions is to shelve them, put them aside, save them for later, or avoid them at all costs. But the Life Brief invites us to dig deep into these questions to find the good stuff waiting within. The juiciest answers come from the most uncomfortable questions.

The Action: Name Your Gripping Issue

All of the other part 1 exercises have been building to this one.

As you reflect on what's bubbled up since you began this journey, take a moment to identify one thing that you want, even if you have no idea whether you can get it, or if you fear that it is out of reach.

You might be doing the dishes or the laundry, and it floats into your mind as a nice daydream that could never come to pass. You may be driving on your commute or a road trip, and boom, it hits you.

I call it "your gripping issue."

Just as my "Mad Love" Brief was about getting to the heart of something I didn't believe was possible, identifying your gripping issue is about giving yourself permission to name a desire you have even if you don't believe it is achievable.

In part 2, we're going to look closely at the writing we've done so far to make sure the gripping issue you identify is one you're ready to explore more deeply, play with, and build a Life Brief around.

But for now, all you need to do is take a moment and reflect on the following questions:

What is one want or theme that keeps coming up? What part or parts of your life are calling for attention? They can be seismic or small. Magnitude doesn't matter, but urgency does.

Now, give your gripping issue a name.

Where is the center of the agitation? What questions around your gripping issue keep showing up? What questions are you avoiding?

It's okay to be gentle.

Go easy. You can acknowledge your discomfort or fear without taking any action. We are simply leaning into curiosity and honesty. Again, no one is watching.

Once you've named your gripping issue, write its name in the center of a piece of paper and draw a circle around it. Then draw rays coming off this circled issue. On each ray write a different way this gripping issue affects your life. Continue drawing as many rays as necessary until you can't think of any more.

Identifying a gripping issue is a bit like unlocking one of the secrets to the universe. Once you identify it, you start to see the way this theme affects *everything*. That's the power it can hold—and why it's so crucial to identify it, challenge it, and explore how to turn it around.

When it came to my original Life Brief, it only took a moment of reflection to see my gripping issue was "time." The word seemed to be screaming at me, making it abundantly clear that the problem wasn't my relationship—it was that I wasn't dedicating enough meaningful *time* to not only my marriage, but myself.

If I were to draw the picture of that first Life Brief, the word **"time"** would be right there in the center of the page in bold and, around it, all the ways I felt time-starved:

- My job is pulling me away from my husband—when we do spend time together, we're delegating, negotiating, arguing.
- I feel so guilty about not having enough time with my family that I'm overcorrecting—every bit of free time I have goes to the kids, and there's none left for me or Chip.
- I've become harsh and critical because I'm giving too much time away, and not spending any time replenishing the well.

Once you can see your gripping issue and hold it in your hand, you can start to connect the dots of its impact on your life.

That's the exploration we'll begin in part 2.

PART 2

GET CLEAR

How are you *feeling*?

"Feeling" is the operative word as we wade into Getting Clear.

Now that we've fearlessly faced our messiness, let's lean into our feelings and intuition and let them lead the way.

Here in part 2 is where you get to practice tuning in to and trusting your intuition. It's normal for this part to feel awkward or uncomfortable, especially at the start.

But when do I write my Life Brief?

We now have the raw ingredients you need to write a Life Brief that is powerful, personal, and actionable. By the time you reach the end of part 2, you will have a Brief that lights you up.

But first we need to make meaning from messiness. We begin the process of Getting Clear by sorting through and reflecting on your writings, extracting the deepest truths from what you've captured. It's from that place of clarity that we'll declare Life Briefs that are boldly honest, sharp, and sticky.

As you've seen from the stories earlier in the book, the process of Getting Clear is iterative, always deepening and unfolding. Sometimes, Briefs come in flashes of certainty, bright and immediate like lightning. Other times, a Brief can percolate, brewing and building before that electricity of aliveness strikes. Then there are Briefs we return to again and again over the course of weeks, or maybe months. There's no right or wrong way. Every Brief, like every person or situation, is different.

As always, enter with ease and a beginner's mindset. Don't rush to a conclusion. See what surfaces when you take a break, step away, or sleep on a question for a night or two.

Go at your own pace and allow yourself to revisit and stir your answers a few times before sinking into the next steps.

Trust that clarity will find you.

CHAPTER 11

LIFE IS A TAPESTRY

I am ready to . . . connect the dots about what I want.

The question: What are my reflections telling me?

The practice: Tap into your knowing.

The action: See Yourself Through a Stranger's Eyes.

A re you feeling overwhelmed by the pile of seemingly disparate threads you've generated from the exercises in part 1? If so, then you share the feeling of every strategist when faced with streams of studies, quotes, and data generated by their exploration phase with a client. *What have I learned? How do I make sense of it? What's critical? What's not? What does it mean?*

What's next?

While there are many principles and frameworks that guide strategists through the brief-development process, there's no precise set of calculations that can be plugged into an algorithm and converted into a tidy strategy. Great results require creative thinking, and creative thinking is a messy affair. The true art of strategy requires reading between the lines of the research, getting curious about emerging themes and patterns, and tapping into your own inner *knowing* to determine how to bring it all together.

Note the distinction I'm making between knowledge—intellectually acquired facts, science, or information—and "knowing," a sharp state of awareness or consciousness. Strategists build up their knowledge in the research stages, exploring their curiosity through observations, interviews, surveys, and science. But strategy is as much of an art as it is a science, and the real strategic magic—the *knowing*—begins once the research is done.

But how do I tap into my knowing?

Allow your feelings to be your guide. In chapter 2, I suggested dedicating a section of your notebook to capture the patterns, themes, aha's, and insights you notice popping up in your writing. If you haven't done so yet, now's the time.

In our next exercise, I'll offer strategies for reflecting on everything you've written, drawn, or doodled since you cracked open these pages. Tune into the emotions that arise as you revisit each of your Brain Dumps, writing entries, and answers to the exercises from part 1. As you read through your reflections, highlight, circle, or underline everything that sparks a notable emotion. Get curious about each emotion—fear, frustration, eagerness, excitement—and take note of its root or source. What's underneath or behind the feeling? Does it come from your ego, or perhaps an attachment to an outdated story or belief, or does it rise from the depths of your soul? And what is it telling you?

As you begin this process of reflection, you will likely notice repetition. Sometimes this will take the form of similar themes in your answers to different questions; other times, you may realize that many answers are circling around the same common threads. Patterns and themes are stepping stones to insights. They are easier to see when you step back and take a higher view.

I liken it to viewing the design of a rug. When you are too close, all you see are lines and threads. But when you stand back from the tapestry, what do you see? What shapes and patterns emerge as you take one step back, then two, then three? Take a 50,000-foot view and survey the entire image.

Insights are a critical part of the brief-writing process—but it takes practice to train yourself to notice and capture them. The textbook definition for insight is an "accurate and deep intuitive understanding about something." In my experience, an insight is a *reveal*. It sheds new light on a subject or situation. It offers a new perspective or way of seeing something familiar. When it comes to our Life Briefs, insights can feel like secrets being confessed. They can show up where you feel the most discomfort or provocation. Don't worry—the next step of the practice will help you tune in to that discomfort and transform it into an action-driven declaration.

When I say the Life Brief is about "tapping into your knowing," I'm inviting you to create space for your insights to emerge. It's not about working hard or thinking harder. At this stage of Getting Clear, it's about stepping back, reflecting on your tapestry, and gazing at the full picture, allowing yourself to see things you may not have noticed before.

Take a nap with them; take a long shower after you read them; go for a walk, run, or drive. See what strikes when you open your mind and invite your truths forward. Take a moment to stand in that open space and absorb the big picture.

The Action:
See Yourself Through a Stranger's Eyes

In this exercise we're going to return to everything we wrote in part 1 with fresh eyes.

It can be an emotional process to revisit our mess. And that's a good thing! We want to feel and take note of the emotions that arise as we start making sense of our messes. They can clue us in to what's important, what provokes us, what scares and excites us.

We also want to step back and think big-picture about what we've discovered. To take this big-picture view, consider borrowing a strategy many writers use during the revision process: reading their writing as if it were someone else's. If you read over your "mess" from a stranger's perspective, what stands out to you? What do you notice when you put some distance between yourself and what you wrote, even if temporarily?

1. Start a new section in your notebook and break out your pen.

2. Aim your attention at the "gripping issue" you identified in chapter 10. Use it as a lens through which you view your reflections. Write **"[your name]'s gripping issue"** at the top of a new page in your notebook.

3. Consider using your name instead of "My" to help you view your gripping issue from a bit of a distance. For example:

BONNIE'S GRIPPING ISSUE:
She wants to spend her time more meaningfully.

BARBARA'S GRIPPING ISSUE:
She wants to stop sacrificing her own needs for the sake of other people.

MARCUS'S GRIPPING ISSUE:
He wants to do work that harnesses his creativity.

4. List any patterns or themes you notice in your Brain Dumps and other writing exercises. Where is there repetition—similar thoughts expressed in different ways or recurring words showing up across exercises? Underline or highlight any words that stand out to you. Do words like "time," "freedom," and "creative" come up? What about themes like "money," "love," "family," and "work"? Highlight recurring words or ideas, write them down in your notebook, and take note of how many times you mention them. More than three is a sign that it's on your mind. If it shows up ten times or twenty (or even more), that's a call for your attention.

BARBARA'S WORDS AND THEMES:

- I say "yes" even when I don't want to and end up feeling resentful.
- I go out of my way to be someone people can count on.
- The words "depleted" or "exhausted" (showed up 15 times in Brain Dumps).
- Things I want for myself are things that energize me—a morning run, working in my garden, nerding out on new recipes.

Capture any aha's or insights that come up. Do your answers reveal something about you or your situation that you hadn't noticed before? Have you experienced any revelations? If so, what are they telling you about what you want? Write it down and capture it all.

Susan, one of my workshop attendees, noticed a theme of "openness" throughout her written reflections about her career. But was she really as open as her Brain Dumps seem to indicate? When she questioned herself deeper, she came to an insight . . . a truth. Susan's "openness" was protecting her from a fear of commitment. As long as she kept herself in a space of ambiguity, she would never have to admit or commit to what she truly desires . . . and would avoid any disappointment or rejection that might come with not getting what she really craves. This insight pushed Susan to keep writing, this time with renewed energy and permission to go deeper and get real.

At the end of this process, you might have several pages that are still a little, well, messy. That's okay because the next exercise will dive deeper into the art of distillation.

CHAPTER 12

THE ART OF DISTILLATION

I choose to . . . get to the heart of what matters to me.

The question: How do I get clear?
The practice: Practice radical distillation.
The action: Separate the Meaningful from the Meaningless.

After decades of authoring creative briefs, I have become a skilled surgeon in separating what matters from what doesn't. Personally, I relish this decluttering process and find it deeply satisfying. Radical distillation means eliminating everything except what's essential to the subject at hand. Turn off the noise, dump the doubts, eliminate the distractions—and finally, you arrive at the core of what you want.

One type of distraction I warn strategists to be on the lookout for are what we call "red herrings"—distractions masquerading as essential, when in actuality they create spin, confusion, or lead us down rabbit holes.

I once worked with a health care company whose mission was to disrupt the traditional medical model of centralized health services—where all doctors and medical services are located near a hospital, requiring patients to drive sometimes long distances to get the medical attention they need. Instead, my clients' company put its clinics next to places where people work and shop, giving patients fast, easy access to quality health care when and where they needed it.

Previous agencies who had worked with this company over-emphasized their spa-like waiting rooms, serene spaces filled with soft colors, calming music, and cucumber water. And it was true—the facilities felt calming and beautiful. But when our agency took the clients through our creative brief process, we focused on the problem they set out to solve: health care services designed around doctors, not patients. A theme that came through every interview with our clients was their pride in designing medical care around how people live—the company was online well before telemedicine became common practice. This was a game changer for people with limited time in their days (aka most of us). At GS&P we named this differentiating and defining quality "Real Life Care."

It turned out that the wonderful amenities in the physical locations were a red herring—they were not the company's essential point of difference. What's more, the emphasis on the facilities had led to the mistaken impression that the company was "too fancy" for the average patient; patients assumed the facilities were out of reach, when in fact the whole point was that they were there to be more accessible.

Remember Marcus from chapter 2? He needed to learn to look past the red herrings of classic success signals (big titles, prominent companies) in order to focus on roles and companies with creativity at their center. He realized he didn't need a company with a prestigious reputation if he was doing work he found meaningful. A big job title was "nice to have" but enjoying his work was a "must have."

I, too, have encountered many red herrings in my Life Brief drafts. Take our Parenting Brief: in the first years of their adolescence, Chip and I were caught up with "managing" our kids' behaviors, and what emerged in our early drafts were a lot of "nice to haves." Kids with steady study habits, good grades, and clean rooms who kept us informed of where they were at all times. But as we moved into getting clear with our Parenting Brief, we realized grades were nice to haves, tidiness wasn't necessary, and that many of the items on our list were not getting to the heart of what truly mattered to us in the "long game" of parenting. What ended up in our Life Brief were the beliefs, roles, and values we wanted to instill: the honesty, responsibility, accountability, self-reliance, and personal agency we were ready to nurture. After much deliberation and distillation, we realized that in instilling these "must haves" we would naturally facilitate the "nice to haves."

Now that you have begun to highlight dominant themes and key threads, let's start sorting and separating what's essential from what's optional, while cutting out the BS, drama, and distractions.

The Action: Separate the Meaningful from the Meaningless

Now is the time to separate the meaningful from the meaningless and meaning-light. What threads can you discard because they cloud the big picture?

When Chip and I wrote our Parenting Brief, our early brainstorms generated everything from music lessons to helping more around the house; more time outside and less time gaming; honoring their word and taking accountability for their actions; us talking less at them and creating more space and connection to hear how they feel. But then we began looking at each item on the list and asking ourselves, *Why?*

Why did we think that clean rooms were important? Why did connection time matter? What meaning were we hoping to instill with each item on the list?

As we pushed ourselves to peel back more layers, we were able to acknowledge that things we thought were must haves were underpinned with deeper meaning. What really mattered to us—seeing, validating, and connecting with them—emerged as the common themes.

As you ask yourself these questions, be ruthlessly and radically honest with your answers. That's how you'll whittle away at distractions until you arrive at the core of what matters most.

One way to sort your threads is to place each in one of three buckets:

1. Must have...
2. Nice to have...
3. Can live without...

Once you have bucketed your thoughts in each of the above categories, take a deeper look at each. Ask yourself, *Why* does this matter? *How* does this address my gripping issue? Is it possible that this item is masking something even deeper?

One useful tool for going deeper is a technique called the Five Whys. Though the practice was first embraced at Toyota as a method of problem-solving, its application has extended far beyond the world of manufacturing. The process is deceptively simple: in order to get to the root cause of a problem—or in this case, desire—we ask *why* five times. For a Toyota engineer, that might have meant, "Why isn't this wheel turning smoothly?"

For the early years of my marriage with Chip, it began with the declaration, "I'm frustrated with my husband."

Why?

"Because he's unhelpful and doesn't pitch in."

Why?

"Because when he does, I skewer him with my criticism."

Why?

"Because I like it done a certain way, and it's important to me for it to be done right."

Why?

"Because I have a hard time letting go of perfection."

I didn't even need the fifth *why* for it to hit me. *Ohhhh*, I thought. *This is not about Chip. It's about me. Maybe my Brief should be about letting go instead of blaming my husband.*

This helped me make the bold declaration: "*I'm ready to kick perfection to the curb.*"

CHAPTER 13

WORD PLAY

I choose to . . . experiment in the search for inspiration.

The question: How do I put what I want into words?
The practice: Play with your words.
The action: Mad Lib Your Mind.

In part 1 we used writing to get the mess out, to practice non-judgment, to uncover all that was hidden. In part 2, we're using writing in a wholly different way. We're distilling through writing. We're using writing to clarify. If part 1 was about stirring the unconscious into consciousness, in part 2, we're getting *very* conscious in an effort to gain clarity.

That's why the words we use matter.

Words are the lifeblood of strategy. Strategies can't exist without them, so strategists are practiced expressionists. We play with the power of words to express ideas that move people into action. A single word choice can make the difference between "meh" and motivating.

Since writing can be daunting for some of us, strategists lean on guiding questions or frameworks as starting points from which to build strategies. The goal is to get to something personal and unforgettable, but we don't have to start with a blank page.

In advertising, we use "thought starters"—ideas from unrelated situations or unexpected contexts—to spark new ideas to get the creative juices flowing. In the context of the Life Brief, thought starters get our engines revving in playful ways, helping us lay down a first set of words that we can use as in the next chapter when we actually (*finally!*) draft our Life Briefs.

A classic marketing framework is called *Get _____ to _____ by_____*, which is essentially a Mad Libs–style framework that helps identify the core building blocks for a marketing strategy. In other words, "Get **(our target audience)** to **(think, feel, or behave differently)** by **(our strategy)**."

Thought starters are playful mechanisms to get our first ideas down on the page—we then use that material like clay, which we will mold, push, and refine. It's a wonderful way to play, create, experiment, and express your Life Brief without pressure.

I'll provide some thought starters later in this chapter, but what I really want you to focus on is the importance of play—to find joy in drafting your Brief so that you can get to declarations that will inspire you (and you alone) into ACTION.

Carmen and Dan learned about the Life Brief not long after the birth of their daughter. They were living in Los Angeles, both working demanding jobs in "hustle culture" industries—Carmen had just returned to a job she described as demanding 99 percent of her, leaving only 1 percent for Dan and their newborn.

Inspired by my original Brief, "Take Our Time," Carmen and Dan set out to do their own writing separately before coming together. When they compared notes, they were surprised to discover lots of similarities: feelings about their current situation—*overstretched, strained, exhausted, beaten down, trapped*; nostalgia for their pre-kid years living in Australia where they relished the balance between work and time together; a vision to raise their daughter as a *global citizen*, instilling an appreciation for different cultures, languages, and ways of life. Dan and Carmen also shared a distaste for LA.

"I don't think of myself as materialistic, but it seeps into you when you're surrounded by it," Carmen told me. "I constantly felt pressure to hustle harder."

"The Life Brief was a catalyst for honest introspection. It was the first time that we had each put something down on paper—the discipline of writing forces you to think about each word, whether you're being honest with yourself. I had to confront what I truly believed before I could share it with Dan."

Carmen's reaction to seeing Dan's Brief was, "Wow, we really are aligned. We can see it right here in writing." There was an aliveness to seeing shared words and ambitions on their individual pages that fueled Carmen and Dan's desire to keep visioning and playing with possibilities. Borrowing language from my original Brief, Dan and Carmen molded and sculpted until they uncovered their own.

- Live a life of fulfillment, focused on things that animate every cell of our being.
- Be a family of global citizens, tasting what the world has to offer through bold excursions.
- Look back and feel that we spent our time well, even when we head down challenging paths.
- Live knowing that the easy and predictable path is not always the most fulfilling one.

One of the secrets of creativity is that while we're aiming for something authentic and unique, we also don't need to reinvent the wheel. The same is true with our Life Briefs—in the next exercise, we're going to get our pens moving with some fill-in-the-blank thought starters. The language is borrowed from my own Briefs to serve as inspiration for yours.

The Action: Mad Lib Your Mind

Here, I take previous Briefs I've written (about relationships, work, self, community or cause, and creativity), removing the keywords of my Briefs and giving you the blanks to fill in with your own answers.

These thought starters lower the "barrier to entry" and initiate the creative thinking process without you having to face a blank page.

As you Mad Lib your mind, remember to play. Try on different answers. See how different words change the meaning of your statements. Use your feelings to guide you on whether your answers are hitting a sweet spot or are way off the mark. Keep playing until you arrive at statements that ring resoundingly true.

Relationship Thought Starters

Fill in the blanks with one specific relationship in mind:

I am ready to _____ and _____ in this relationship. I choose to feel _____ and _____ with this person. I choose to be more _____ and _____ when we are together.

Work Thought Starters

Fill in the blanks while thinking of your job—
remember, this doesn't need to be your current job:

I am ready to walk a path of _____, not just _____. I choose to _____ to get to my fullest potential. I choose to do work that _____ and _____. I want to activate _____ in others. I am ready to influence people in _____ and _____ ways.

118

Self Thought Starters

Fill in the blanks while thinking about
what you want to give to yourself:

I choose to experience _____ and _____ daily. I'm ready to embrace _____ and overcome _____. I am ready to start _____ and stop _____. I choose to create space for _____ and _____. I choose to nurture and nourish _____ and _____.

Community or Cause Thought Starters

Fill in the blanks for your commitment to your community or cause:

I'm fired up to _____ and _____. I choose to deepen my devotion to _____. I choose to serve in _____ and _____ ways. I am ready to give more of my _____ and _____.

Creativity Thought Starters

Fill in the blanks while thinking about what
you want to give to your creative life.

I am _____, and I'm ready to unlock my _____. I choose to _____ without restraint. I'm ready to harness my _____ and lean into _____ in order to unleash the full force of my creative aliveness.

CHAPTER 14

DECLARE YOURSELF

I am ready to . . . be explicit about what I really want.

The question: What else do I need to write my Life Brief?

The practice: Declare what you want.

The action: The Five Declarations.

Did you notice anything about the way the thought starters from the previous chapter began?

I am . . .

I choose . . .

I'm ready . . .

In order to unearth meaning, we began each commitment with a powerful declaration, rooted in the here and now. Not a wish or a hope aimed at some distant future.

Declarations are firm and affirmative, present, in the moment. When you read them, they ooze with conviction and commitment. Their power and purpose are to plant what you want solidly in the "now," not in the ambiguous "later." *These* are the kinds of meaty, take-no-prisoners statements we want in our Life Briefs.

Remember that great Briefs are short. They express the essence of things so that you have the crystal clarity to act. Start with a declaration of what you're ready to activate—not what you want tomorrow, but what you boldly choose today, what you're ready to have your life look like right now. The goal is to be simple yet generative, truthful yet inspiring.

Declarations are full of energy: commitment expressed with feeling.

With that in mind, it's time to translate the pieces we've collected throughout the book so far into our very first Life Brief.

The Action: The Five Declarations

Aim your attention at the "gripping issue" you identified at the end of part 1—a topic you feel called to write a Life Brief about in this very moment.

If your focus is on a relationship with someone you care about, tune in to that person, and see them in your mind's eye. If it's your work that you want to reimagine, visualize yourself doing the work you dream about. If the Brief is about your connection to self or community, visualize the future you want to bring into being.

Whatever you decide, make sure it's something that lights you up.

First, meditate on the insights you've collected. Drop into your quiet. Get your trusty pen and notebook, your notes app, or even the pages of this book.

Your next step? Distill everything you have discovered, uncovered, and unlocked into five declarative sentences, much like the ones you played with in the previous chapter's Mad Libs exercise. If you want to carry over any statements from your Mad Libs, go right ahead.

Be ruthless with your distillation. Let go of anything that you think you *should* want, or that someone else wants for you. This is YOUR Brief and yours alone. Capture what matters most to YOU in this arena of your life—what YOU want to realize; how YOU want to feel and experience it. You're creating a living, breathing document, and in this stage, we're focused on honesty and meaning. We'll continue pushing and refining the words in the coming chapters.

Remember the power of declarations—start your sentences with "I'm ready" or "I choose" rather than "I wish" or "I hope."

Full disclosure: my first Life Brief wasn't as declarative as the ones I've written in later years. I've since realized how much bolder I feel when I choose declarative words—words that give me a feeling of agency. Words that make me think, *I've got this.*

I am ... I choose ... I'm ready ...

This is how we set ourselves up to activate our Briefs in part 3.

THE LIFE BRIEF FIRST DRAFT:
YOUR FIVE DECLARATIONS

• I am _____

_____

_____

_____

_____

• I choose _____

_____

_____

_____

_____

• I'm ready _____

_____

_____

_____

CHAPTER 15

PUSH YOUR BRIEF

I choose to . . . go beyond my comfort zone.

The question How do I know when my Brief is done?

The practice: Take it to "Fuck Yes."

The action: Push Your Life Brief 3x.

If you've drafted a Life Brief you feel lukewarm about, you'll never gather up the energy you need to put it into practice.

Wait. That wasn't quite right. Let me rephrase that.

> *If you're not excited about your Life Brief,*
> *you're never going to put it into action.*

Closer. Let's give it one more try. Here goes . . .

Your Life Brief should
make you feel
"FUCK YES."

That's it. That's the point I was trying to make. It just took me a couple of tries to get it right.

That's the work we're doing now—the work of revision and refinement. And once again, we're using writing to guide us forward.

"Writing is rewriting," says journalist Donald Murray. In other words, revision is not only about correcting or polishing—it's an essential part of the writing process.

Once you have identified your Five Declarations—the first draft of your Brief—you can shape, sharpen, and embolden it. Now that it's captured in writing, you can reread each sentence and ask yourself, *Does it ring true? Does it capture the fullness of what I want? Does it excite me? Can it be bolder? Can it be more vivid? Is it specific enough?* If not, what's missing? What's still not quite right? What can you do to take it from *meh* to *Fuck Yes*?

I discovered the power of pushing my Life Brief with "Mad Love." For that iteration of my Marriage Brief, I first played with writing, "I'm ready to stop fighting with Chip," "I'm ready to get along," and "I choose to be a more generous and gracious partner." Those are truthful statements and valid desires, but they're too practical and safe to be Life Briefs.

The full truth was deeper than just wanting to get along. The full truth was that I wasn't ready to stop being a sexual being. Just getting along felt like robbery. It didn't excite me, and it certainly didn't light me up. Of course I wanted to get along, but that wasn't *all* of what I wanted or longed for from my marriage. It wasn't the deepest distillation of what would truly be meaningful. I needed to get more honest and even brazen with myself—admit what I craved. What I wanted was mad love, even if writing it down terrified me because I didn't believe that it was possible. I wanted—and continue to want—to be in *mad love* with Chip. It wasn't enough to just *get along*. Yet, it took me reviewing and revising my Brief multiple times to admit something that might shatter me if it didn't come to fruition.

What do I want so badly that it would shatter me if I never allowed it into my life?

When you read your Five Declarations, do you feel at peace, or are you still turning something over? When you look into your heart of hearts, do you feel that you're holding back, or that you've nailed it? Is any piece of the Brief not sitting right with you? Perhaps you're thinking, *No, that's not the word. It's just off by an inch*—or *by a mile.* Now that you've written it, take the time to sit with it and contemplate what has poured out.

I've found that most Briefs get better when I take more than one pass. (That's why this chapter's exercise will walk you through "pushing your Brief 3x.") Sometimes the pushes happen in a single sitting. Other times, I revisit a Brief over days or even weeks, rereading it at regular intervals, checking for the Fuck Yes–ness of each declaration. If I don't feel it, I keep pushing and playing with it.

The test of rewriting is, can you be even more honest with yourself in each draft? Can you sharpen the language and make it more evocative? More descriptive? More colorful and emotive? Can you make it bolder? Can you take yourself to the edge of nervousness? Because what nervousness often means is, *I really do want it, but I don't know that it's possible.*

Here is one important thing to note. We live in a society where we often confuse "more" and "bigger" with "bolder," and so when I ask you to be "bold and brave," that might sound like "go bigger," or "be more ambitious."

That's not what I mean. Sometimes the boldest thing we can do is to pull back and slow down. Boldness is not always about going for big trophies. Boldness is about pushing your Brief to the edges of your comfort zone, in whatever terms make sense to you. For some of you that might mean putting yourself out further into the world, daring to go for more than you've let yourself believe you can have. For others, it might mean changing directions and finding a new path that feels "quieter" but is infinitely more satisfying than the one that you're on.

In advertising, we tell clients: if the creative work doesn't make you nervous, it's probably not going to work. Advertising is the art of captivating attention and igniting action. These are big challenges when you're working in fractions of time—sixty seconds, fifteen seconds, and now even six seconds of time. Each person's attention is pulled this way and that thousands of times each day—hundreds of times an hour. It's near impossible to be memorable amidst that barrage. But in advertising, invisibility and indifference are failure, and so the strategist must issue a call to action so compelling that all who hear it take note.

In the same way, writing your Life Brief is about boldly activating *you*. It's about stirring something deeply within *you*.

Holding back and playing it safe is a direct path to forgettable and is guaranteed to fail.

Let's go deeper.

The Action: Push Your Life Brief 3x

In this exercise, you're going to take the first draft of your Brief (your Five Declarations from the previous chapter) and rewrite it three times to push your Life Brief to the deepest, boldest, sharpest place possible.

Push 1: Go Deeper

In this first push, let's see where we can get nakedly honest about what we want. Read each of your Five Declarations and ask yourself, *Is this true? Where am I holding back? What am I resisting or avoiding? What am I still shy about admitting? What have I left off the table?*

Now, rewrite your Five Declarations, getting more honest and stripping away any hesitation.

- I am _____
  _____
  _____
  _____
  _____

- I choose _____
  _____
  _____
  _____
  _____

- I'm ready _____
  _____
  _____
  _____
  _____

Push 2: Be Bolder

This is where you moon-shot your Brief. In other words, allow yourself to dream and get beyond realism. Set aside that internal voice begging you to see *how* you'll get there.

One way to dream big is to wonder "what if...?" This is an easy, risk-free way for you to open your mind up to daydreaming and playing with possibilities, while quieting your inner realist.

Review your Five Declarations. Allow yourself to ponder on "what if..." for each statement. Stretch and challenge yourself to push to the edges of your imagination. Write a "what if..." for each of your Five Declarations.

Here are examples of "what if..." statements applied to one of my central themes, Time:

"WHAT IF . . ."

- What if I give myself two hours of unadulterated, dedicated "me time" every week?
- What if I flipped the hours I spend on my agency job with the time I spend with Chip, our kids, and the stuff that lights me up?
- What if I work on my job for a "season" (a few concentrated months each year), and spend the rest of the year with our family and my passions?

Now you try:

"WHAT IF . . ."

_____

_____

_____

_____

Now reread your Five Declarations. Ask yourself, *Where am I playing it safe?* Remove anything that hedges your bets—and add in anything you've edited out because you can't yet see how it's possible. Revisit your "what if . . ." statements and use them to inspire this push.

List your Five Declarations again, making each statement bolder and braver.

- I am _____

_____

_____

_____

_____

- I choose _____
  _____
  _____
  _____
  _____

- I'm ready _____
  _____
  _____
  _____
  _____

Push 3: Get Sharper

Now we're going to sharpen your words. An idea expressed one way can feel ho-hum. The same idea written differently can have a radically inspiring effect. Because the best Briefs motivate and move people (in this case, YOU) into action, they use words that are rich in meaning. Meaning is loudest when it's specific and pointed, not vague or broad.

As you look at each line in your Brief, ask yourself, does it light you up with aliveness? Do your words give you goose bumps? Do they spark a fire in your belly? Do they take you to the edge of excited nervousness? That's when you know you've nailed it. I rewrote my Mad Love Brief to make it more ambitious and more vivid until I had the Brief that was bold enough to make me nervous, a moon shot that simultaneously energized and terrified me: *I choose to get along → I'm ready to feel and express our love to one another again → I'm ready to* **fall madly in love** *with my husband again.*

On the next page, list your Five Declarations one final time, making each statement sharper and more vivid.

THE LIFE BRIEF

- I am _____
  _____
  _____
  _____
  _____

- I choose _____
  _____
  _____
  _____
  _____

- I'm ready _____
  _____
  _____
  _____
  _____

CHAPTER 16

GIVE IT A HANDLE— NAME YOUR BRIEF

I am ready to . . . get single-minded.

The question: How do I remember my Brief?
The practice: Get sharp and sticky.
The action: The T-Shirt Test.

Now that you've put your Five Declarations through the wringer, it's time to get single-minded and sticky with your message.

At the heart of every Life Brief is a single phrase or handle that you can use to sum up the thought, work, and play that you've put into this practice. It can act as a reminder, a reinforcement, and a shorthand whenever you need a gut check. Words really do matter here, so make yours sing. The shorter and sharper this line is, the more memorable and motivating it will be.

This chapter is about capturing the essence of your Brief in a way that's unshakable to you, so that it's always there when you need it. What we're looking for here is a phrase that captures the whole meaning of your Five Declarations in one line. This one line—your Brief's handle—is the key that unlocks the treasure trove of your Life Brief; this way, you don't need to walk around with your pages of writing to return to the place of clarity that brought you here.

When I'm in a work meeting and a racial equity issue arises, I remember "Relations, Not Just Solutions"; this helps me stay present with my intentions and lean into my Life Brief in that moment. When I feel the sting of lack, or pressure to choose work over family, I tune in to my Wealth Brief, "Be Rich in Relationship." Each time I do this, I feel a sense of calm returning—this is how I know that my Brief is still serving me.

It's more important for your handle to be captivating than comprehensive or even technically correct. We see this in the advertising industry every day. Think of iconic ad campaigns like "got milk?" It was a risk for the California Milk Processor Board to choose an irreverent, grammatically incorrect tagline—but it stuck, precisely because it was so awkward. Jeff Goodby and Rich Silverstein, the masterminds behind "got milk?" played with a number of safer, still technically "good" taglines along the way, but none had the sticking power of that now legendary question. It is one of the most famous taglines ever to exist in advertising. Today, decades after its launch, I still run across stickers, signs, and T-shirts hijacking Jeff's infamous line, hawking everything from sleep aids to plumbing to pest control.

The strategy for "got milk?" hinged on the insight that people only think about milk when they've run out of it. It's such a simple yet meaningful insight because up until that point, the advertising was telling people, "Milk does a body good."

Since when do humans always do what's good for them?

When you see a giant thirty-foot peanut butter and jelly sandwich on a billboard with the phrase "got milk?," on the other hand, it's hard not to salivate. The visceral memory of peanut butter stuck to the roof of your mouth can't be solved with a soda or energy drink. Nope. Not even a glass of water will do. You immediately think of a tall glass of milk. The phrase "got milk?" was just awkward enough to imprint on our minds. They could have said, "Run out of milk?," "Need more milk?," or "Replace the milk," but none of those would have the sticking power of that iconically awkward phrase.

We wrap our Life Briefs in a single-minded, sticky handle so that we'll always remember how we want to live. I can't recite all five lines of my Marriage Brief in the heat of the moment, but "Mad Love" is an easy prompt to focus on the big picture. And when I say "Mad Love" to Chip, he instantly knows what I mean. The sticky handle is how you keep your Life Brief alive in your mind. You don't have to put a reminder in your phone; you don't have to put a Post-it Note on your bathroom mirror. When you say the phrase, your mind shifts into gear with understanding and a call to action.

That is advertising's superpower—tattooing an idea in our minds. It's why my son used to sing insurance jingles in the car. It's why advertising clients spend millions of dollars in media, always with the same question in mind: *Can it permeate the minds of people, of culture at large, get people to adopt the idea and make it their own?* That's the art of creative strategy. Helping us get to that moment, that springboard, that then cracks open and unleashes ideas, decisions, and actions.

We want the Life Brief to have the same resonance.

The most vivid expression of your Life Brief—the word or phrase that embodies the fullness of the life you want to live—is often the most memorable. And so, the handle for your Brief may already be right in front of you. What you're looking for is a phrase that sums it all up. You're not looking to be clever just for the sake of it. You are looking for stickiness—memorability. If there is a song title or a lyric that perfectly illustrates your Life Brief, don't be afraid to use it. You don't have to be the original author of the phrase.

As long as it lights you up, that's your handle.

The Action: The T-Shirt Test

Say your handle out loud. How does it feel? Say it aloud again, changing any words until you land on the phrase that is most sticky. Remember, memorability is key.

Can you imagine it as a hashtag or on a bumper sticker? How about a T-shirt? Think about some of the most memorable T-shirts you've seen. "The future is female," or "Keep it simple, stupid." Short, powerful, and sticky enough for the front (or back) of a T-shirt.

Jeff Goodby invites us to be vandals in service of creativity—to break rules and borrow from culture and the world at large, no matter how far afield it may seem. Look around you; there are signs everywhere. If your Life Brief was captured by a song or set of lyrics, which would it be? Do you see art around you that could inspire the name of your Brief, something that personifies your vision of what life could be? Is there a meme that sums it up?

Your Brief's handle should be a word or phrase that has staying power. It should call up the fullness of your Brief in one thought, one that never leaves you. You know you've hit it right on the head when you have something that you'd put on a T-shirt—something that captures the essence of your Brief bravely, boldly, and clearly.

Stop.

Do not go any further.

Not yet . . .

If your single-minded Life Brief handle

and your Five Declarations

don't make you feel

"FUCK YES,"

go back to chapter 15.

If—*and only if*—your Life Brief lights you up, turn the page . . .

PART 3

GET ACTIVE

You did it. You've written your first Life Brief. Take this moment to celebrate yourself!

Not only is your Life Brief an accomplishment in its own right, but it's also your first action—an act of commitment, an act of movement and momentum. So let's build on that momentum. Let's use the ideas and exercises in part 3 to fan the fire in your belly. Now that you've gotten clear, it's time to activate your Life Brief. Time to embark on creative, courageous, no-regrets living.

So how exactly does a Life Brief make a different kind of living possible?

In my advertising work, creative briefs expand the field of possibility for how a company shows up and interacts in the world. Once a creative brief has been expressed, a palpable excitement fills the air. It's a suspended moment of time where ideas begin to stir and anything feels possible.

It is also a period of suspense. Now that we have expressed the bold purpose and ambition for a brand—what happens next?

As any strategist will tell you, briefs are useless unless they catalyze action. A Brief is not meant to stay on the page, it's meant to inspire a company's next move, and a hundred more actions after that. It's there to help a team decide what to focus on, and what to ignore. It's a bit like a compass for the way forward, a scalpel to cut through the thickets, a light in the dark.

So how do we use this indispensable tool to move from possibility into action? How do get from where we are now to where we want to be? How do we go from creative dreaming to creative living?

It's time to find out.

A final word before we dive into part 3. The last thing I want is for you to feel like you need to start "doing" more. Your Life Brief is not meant to feel like (or turn into) a second job. What follows are stories and strategies to guide you—through moments where you feel stuck, begin to second-guess, or find yourself at a crossroads. But these ideas and practices are not busywork, they're not steps to be followed in order, and they're not homework assignments you're going to be graded on.

Remember, a Life Brief is a practice, not a plan.

Your Life Brief shows you a path forward that is uniquely yours, a way of being that only you can express. Yes, you're officially off-roading now, but you're not doing so recklessly. You have connected to your inner truth. You have expressed it in a way that is sticky, sharp, and activating. Now is the exciting part—when you get to turn the wheel over to your Life Brief and let it drive you forward.

Let's see what unfolds.

CHAPTER 17

ALLOW YOUR BRIEF
TO SURPRISE YOU

I choose to . . . open myself to what shows up.

The question: How do I unlock real change?
The practice: Let your Life Brief unfold.
The action: Say Yes to Serendipity.

Amazing things start to happen once you have clarity.
From our very first Life Brief, Chip and I learned that once we get clear about what we want, unexpected twists and unimaginable rewards begin to reveal themselves. Soon after we penned that original Brief, the stars seemed to align. Chip called me with an online ad for a big, colorful house at the heart of a vibrant values-driven community we had discovered while vacationing in Portland, Oregon, two years earlier.

Wait . . . I know this house!

During that vacation, we had found ourselves drawn to and openly admiring an intersection at the heart of a community where neighbors had painted a gigantic sunflower street mural. We had noticed that on one of its corners stood a grand Victorian house, painted in red, fronted by a colorful mosaic water fountain and arches declaring "Sunnyside Piazza." Now, two years after that trip, our Life Brief was bringing us back to this *very same house.*

The serendipity didn't end there. In my research for progressive public schools, one school kept coming up—an environmentally driven, service-centered school that happened to be in Portland. When Chip came across the online ad for the house, we were stunned to find out that the school I had researched was just one block away.

This was only weeks after we'd pledged to act on and honor our Life Brief at all costs, against all fears.

Yet, when the opportunity to move to Portland—to swiftly seize our Life Brief—presented itself, we hesitated. "Is this *really* what we want? Are we seriously going to go for it?" There was a clear expiration date on this opportunity; people were already on the waiting list to rent this house that we instinctively and immediately loved. Yes, we could see that the house would allow us to take the first real leap towards the life we wanted and imagined.

But there was still a lot of uncertainty around this decision. Some part of us was suspended in disbelief that our Life Brief could tangibly realize itself so soon—only months after writing it and accepting our radical new vision for our lives. Each step—from answering the Craigslist post to applying for the house—felt as if we were "role-playing change." Like, somewhere along the way, a door would close, and we would be turned back to the safety and sameness of the life we were already living. *Do we really want to leave our community in Petaluma and move to Portland?* we asked ourselves frantically. *What are we doing? Are we crazy?* The doubts came flooding in, as did the urge to backpedal and stop the train.

Armed with only intuition and zero guarantees, we decided to *just say yes.* We took the leap towards fulfilling our Brief. We put in an application, gathered artifacts of our family—photos of our kids, our wedding vows, our Life Brief—to persuade the owners that we would be the best fit for their home, that we would love, grow, and care for it just as they had. We put it all in a box and sent it off, hoping that though we were fourth in line, our heartfelt plea would sway them. Soon, we got the call. We were moving to Oregon.

We flew to Portland to view the house in person and encountered another moment of surprise and serendipity. We'd seen the outside of the house during our vacation and loved it, but we had never toured its interior, even after signing the rental lease. The vibrant Victorian exterior didn't fit my modern and minimalist personal style, but I told myself to let go of that and appreciate everything else it had to offer—the spaciousness for our growing family, a values-driven community, walking distance to the kind of school we wanted for our kids.

As we entered, we were shocked to discover an interior that was everything I had dreamed of. The house was open and fresh on the inside, and in complete opposition to its exterior. Blond wood, white walls, exposed beams, soaring ceilings, modern and stunning. "Are you kidding me?" I was floored.

We walked to the corner of the block to find a cupcake shop and home goods store just steps away from our new house. On the next corner, Stumptown Coffee Roasters, perfect for Chip's coffee obsession. In between, a pizza parlor, breakfast café, and a diner that our kids would love. Across the street, a grocery store for ease and convenience when our days already felt so jam-packed. A block in the other direction was the environmentally driven, community-centered school. It felt as if we had won some special kind of lottery. Everything we needed and wanted was right there, perfectly laid out for the needs of our family.

But wait.

I had this big job at the agency I loved in California. I had been there for so long—through the births of my children and the upward trajectory of my career—that I couldn't imagine leaving. I led the biggest accounts there. What was I going to do for work if I left? If I quit, we'd have no income. Chip was building his own documentary company, which demanded time, energy, and expense. In that moment, I was our sole breadwinner. On top of that, I was still doing the lion's share of caring for our three young kids. This imbalance had already been a major source of strain in our relationship. Now we were thinking of adding more financial pressure with the move. How would we do it? How could we? Were we being irresponsible parents? Was this too big a leap? The terror of reality set in as our Life Brief became tangible and no longer hypothetical.

I summoned my courage and went to see the president of our agency.

"I love this place and its people. There is no agency like it. But my family needs a seismic shift in our lives, so we're moving to Oregon," I told him, fighting back tears. I knew that this was what I needed to do for my life as a whole, but it was an emotional conversation. "I'm here to give my notice."

Derek didn't bat an eye. Instead, in the kind of surprise gift that I've come to receive over and over again when inviting in the world through a Life Brief, he said, "Why don't you do your job from Portland?"

Once again, I was floored. At the time, remote work was unprecedented—and certainly unheard of in our company. Not only that, but I'd already resigned myself to quitting. I had braced myself for trade-offs, loss even. I was willing to sacrifice my job in pursuit of our Life Brief. I was ready to let go.

But Derek offered me the gift of a scenario I hadn't even considered: my clients wouldn't care where I was based. Working from home was an option. I had been so mired in my concern about the problem that I had not even entertained the notion that there might be alternative solutions beyond the either-or scenario in my mind.

Derek's offer jolted me into realizing that my mind had me playing small. My limited beliefs about the options available to me drove me to assume that quitting was the only way forward. I had deeply dug into my values and decided that I was willing to trade my beloved job for a chance to realize our Life Brief. It wasn't until I acted on my Brief that previously unimagined solutions fell into view.

Each time I have written a Life Brief and pledged to live by it, the unexpected happens, offering me something even better than I could have planned.

When you let go of your fears, and surrender to what you really want, you open yourself up to unexpected twists. Commit to the vision you have of what you want and allow the world to join you. I have been astonished by the unimaginable gifts of surprise and serendipity that accompany a more creative way of living—both in my own life, and in the lives of those who have adopted the Life Brief as their new operating premise.

This is why I no longer plan the big strokes of my life, why my primary focus is clarity, commitment through writing, and conscious, courageous actions. I allow things to show up that I could not anticipate or plan for, even if I tried.

When we try to plan every step, we end up confined by our limiting beliefs of how far others will go to support and enable us. We end up missing the delicious invitations that can open up around us when we follow our vision without attachments. When we commit to our Life Brief, we give the world permission to join us.

The Action: Say Yes to Serendipity

Have you encountered moments in your life when the stars seemed to suddenly align? Or times when you gave in to a moment of fantasy, only to have it realized unexpectedly? How do you react in those moments? Do you welcome and embrace them with abandon and relish? Do you approach them with hesitation and caution? Or do you outright dismiss them and move on?

When Chip called me about the online ad for the Sunnyside Piazza house, I was faced with two choices:

- Say, "Yes, let's find out more."
- Dismiss it, forget it, and move on.

Life is a Choose Your Own Adventure. These choices are always available and yours to make. With your Brief in hand, how will you meet your next invitation or opportunity differently? What are you ready to embrace that you used to dismiss?

How will you respond to your next unexpected invitation or unanticipated opportunity? Instead of dismissing it or moving on out of doubt or disbelief, name three ways you will receive it.

1. _____
   _____
   _____

2. _____
   _____
   _____

3. _____
   _____
   _____

CHAPTER 18

ACTION IS A BY-PRODUCT OF CLARITY

I'm ready to . . . redirect my attention.

The question: Which way do I go?

The practice: Your Brief is your guide.

The action: Use Your Brief as a Springboard and Filter.

Action is a by-product of clarity.

Clarity focuses your attention and centers your intentions in ways that generate waves of momentum towards something bigger. It automatically attunes us to what matters most, making it easier to act.

Sounds simple, right? It is, until we remember how easily our attention gets hijacked by everything else in our lives—requests, responsibilities, other people's dramas, "sleepwalking" habits born of boredom and restlessness.

Clarity is the knife that cuts through it all.

Armed with the clarity of your Life Brief, all you need to realign your attention and actions is to take it out and reconnect with it. Remember:

the role of a creative brief is to provide a sharp yet expansive strategy that propels a brand forward into the future. The Life Brief aims to do the same for you.

A Life Brief is especially useful when you find yourself in an utterly unfamiliar moment. It can guide you through uncertainty, as it did for Aaron, a young finance exec who was thrust into a stressful and destabilizing period after suddenly losing his job.

For years, Aaron lived abroad, working in his dream job—one that provided his young family with the adventure and lifestyle he and his wife had long craved. Singapore was their base, but Aaron's job afforded him the flexibility to bring his wife and son along on work trips to Shanghai and Hong Kong, while touring Vietnam and the Maldives on weekends and holidays.

Everything seemed to click, until Aaron's company suddenly merged with another, and he was laid off with the rest of their Singapore office. Without employment, Aaron and his family would lose their visas—and as the clock ticked, Aaron began to panic, lining up every possible interview he could with companies in the region.

Each interview sent his hopes skyrocketing, but after a number of dead ends, time ran out.

After he got the call that the final position he'd applied for had been filled, Aaron went upstairs to the bedroom in hopes of hiding his shame from his family. Climbing onto the bed, he collapsed into himself, his tears turning into convulsions. The sobs were too loud to suppress. He recalls seeing his wife's face, stunned, not knowing what to say or do. "In my head I was screaming, *I'm a failure. I failed you. I failed our family.*"

After they moved back to Houston, the family of three stayed with his in-laws and slept in his wife's childhood bedroom. Aaron fell into a depression. They had to sell, donate, or box up into storage most of their possessions. They spent the holidays hibernating from the world, turning down invitations to see friends and extended family. They were burning through their savings. Friends offered to help, but Aaron declined, determined to be self-reliant.

"I'm supposed to be able to provide for this family. Goddamn, I should be able to do this. If I can't, that is my own moral shortcoming."

Losing his job had triggered Aaron's long-held beliefs about who he was supposed to be and how he should show up for himself, at work, and for his loved ones. He had been raised to have a plan and be on a path at all times—know what he was doing and where he was going next. It was not okay to have moments of question or doubt. It was not okay to not be okay.

Aaron threw himself into the job hunt once more, shooting at anything, grasping for straws. He chased every lead and job posting with a big salary that could allow him to reclaim what he thought of as his former glory. He had a few conversations with companies, but there was little movement.

For the first time ever, it seemed, he had no idea what to do next.

It was around this time that Aaron discovered the Life Brief. The idea of seeing his life through a beginner's mind and approaching his struggles with curiosity was a revelation. Aaron put pen to paper and captured his thoughts. He allowed his questions to push beyond what he wanted his next job to pay or what he wanted it to say about him. He pressed himself to think deeper about how he wanted to feel in the role. As he wrote, something clicked.

The job he lost represented an identity and level of success that had been important to him, and he had molded himself to fit that identity. He was embarrassed by what he deemed a failure. He wanted to save face and provide for his family the way his previous job had allowed him to do. But in his scramble to reascend the ladder, Aaron realized he was jumping at everything, unfocused and depleted. He didn't have any search criteria in place other than "available" and "fast."

As he distilled his thoughts down to what he really wanted, he remembered an old adage about the art of saying no to things that aren't right for you so that you can say yes to fewer, better things. That "aha" propelled Aaron to shift his shotgun approach to one of intentional focus. Instead of adapting himself to each job posting, Aaron shifted his focus to what *he wanted* from the job and company. Rather than molding himself to be a cookie-cutter version of what he thought these companies were looking for, Aaron centered on becoming a first-rate version of himself.

Soon, an opportunity appeared that excited him. Aaron was asked to come to the office to present examples of his past work, which he had at the ready from past interviews. But this time, Aaron adapted his presentation to be more casual, more conversational, more personal and true to who he was in private. Instead of trying to be the perfect candidate who oozed evidence of his background with every word, Aaron concentrated on telling his story, his way, sharing a more personal point of view. "It was a big room, with two founders, the CEO, COO, and CMO. I remember clicking through the slides and thinking, *This is actually pretty fucking good.* I could see them smiling and nodding. When I finished, the CEO came over and gave me a solid handshake, thanking me for coming in. I got the offer later that day."

Landing the job was just the beginning of Aaron's shift. Whereas past coworkers used to describe Aaron as "intellectual," current colleagues describe him as "real." The feedback he had received in past performance reviews was consistent—*Aaron is very smart. He's doing all the right things, but he talks at us. He condescends. It feels like he's reading from a script.*

Aaron had been trying so hard to live up to the expectations he assumed people had for him, that he had never allowed himself to fully be himself. "I was profoundly insecure. I thought that if I hid behind these pyramids, charts, and templates, maybe no one would notice. If I filled a big house with tons of stuff, maybe that would make me feel worthy.

When I stripped the charts away and found a way to tell stories I cared about, I was able to connect to people and get them to care about those stories, too."

Aaron has sustained his shift in focus. His Life Brief practice reminds him to play to his strengths instead of worrying about how he might fall short in other people's eyes. He continues to say no to things that don't feel right so that he can focus on what truly matters. And he has since "Life Briefed" more than just his work. He and his wife have purged their home and closets—from furniture to clothes to photos. They are committed to having fewer but better things that they care for and love. They prioritize time spent together. Aaron goes to work earlier so that he can be home sooner. They choose to rent instead of taking on the stresses of home ownership. Saying no to those stressors has created space for Aaron to say yes to being a better partner, father, and friend.

Life Briefs help people filter out the irrelevant while actively prioritizing the important.

How can you use your Life Brief to aim your attention—and your actions—towards where you want to go?

The Action: Use Your Brief as a Springboard and Filter

Create an evening ritual of revisiting your Brief. Draw your focus and attention to your Life Brief as you reread it, allowing each word, each sentence, to penetrate deeply into your consciousness. Breathe it in.

Now look at your next day's schedule and ask yourself, *Does my day align with my Brief? If not, what can I adapt or adjust? What am I choosing out of habit? Where can I inject more intention?*

Rewrite your schedule according to priority, instead of chronology. List each activity or action item in order of what matters most.

1. Which actions are "must do"?
2. Which are "want to do"?
3. Which "can wait for later"?

Of course not everything you do needs to be in service of your Life Brief. But it does become an easy and clarifying filter for eliminating distractions and drama when you're ready to roll up your sleeves and dig in.

As more of my Life Briefs centered on time, I began to review and reimagine the ways I spend my time. By examining the patterns around my relationship to time, I realized two things. First, if I don't actively block out time for what matters most, other people will fill that time. And second, much of my time was dominated by busywork, or "nice to do" versus "must do" and "love to do." These two aha's prompted me to shift my approach to schedules at work and responses at home, in service of my Brief.

A simple framework for making deliberate shifts is called Start, Stop, Shift.

- What are you ready to START doing, in service of your Life Brief?
- What are you ready to STOP doing?
- What habits or behaviors are you ready to SHIFT?

BONNIE'S START, STOP, SHIFT

START: Start blocking out short bursts of time in my daily schedule for myself (space for breaks and breathers) and my Brief (for research or writing or responding to invitations).

ACTION IS A BY-PRODUCT OF CLARITY

STOP: Stop saying yes to calls, meetings, or requests where I don't play an essential role.

SHIFT: Reframe my perspective around productivity. See that spaciousness is just as important as "doing"— or better yet, that spaciousness is key to productivity.

CHAPTER 19

STEP INTO CREATIVE LIVING

I am ready to . . . move into action.

The question: How do I propel myself forward?

The practice: Harness your aliveness.

The action: Chase Your Goose Bumps.

Throughout this book, we've used creative tools and prompts to get us closer to our inner truth. We've employed creative thinking to help us rewrite limiting beliefs. But I want to talk for a moment about just what I mean when I say that the Life Brief is a pathway to "creative, courageous living." And I want to share why a creative mindset can be a potent tool as you Get Active.

Life itself is a creative act. Unfortunately, most of us have not been invited to see things that way—perhaps we think of creativity as something available only to people who work in a creative field or have an artistic hobby. But creativity is not a skill, it's a mindset.

How do we cultivate such a mindset? And why is it essential to the Life Brief journey?

I'm lucky and deeply grateful to have spent my entire adult life surrounded by wizards of creativity—people driven by a thirst to find a better way, experiment with what can be, try what's never been done before. Creativity is the oxygen I have breathed for over three decades now. It's intoxicating and deeply satisfying to harness the power of creativity to change minds, hearts, and behaviors; to permeate and shape culture; to move companies, people, and at times society, forward.

The secret of how this happens is actually quite simple. Creative people don't see "impossible." The word isn't in their vocabulary. I know, I know, it sounds cliché—the stuff of motivational posters. But in my experience, wildly creative people are idea-led—they're driven by a velocity of vision that doesn't allow them to accept no for an answer. That's not how most people operate: many of us are taught to be "realistic." If we can't see the "how," we dismiss or reject the idea. Frankly, I find few things more frustrating than to be told to be "practical" or "realistic," especially when I'm pumped about an idea. "Realistic" is what people say when they're pushing their limiting beliefs on you.

Creative people do the opposite.

When they're fired up by an idea, they do *everything* in their capacity to make it real. They round up and rally their allies and teammates. They dive into research and they gather resources. They're as creative about finding new approaches to making an idea a reality as they are about coming up with ideas in the first place.

Think of your Life Brief as the permission to do the same.

Allow your Brief—and the energy around it—to be so big that you'll do whatever it takes to figure out your way forward. Let yourself be led by the idea, the vision, the dream—not by the road (or roadblocks) to realizing it.

How often do we fall into the trap of abandoning or tamping down something we want when we can't see every step of the journey? When was the last time you let uncertainty—terror of the unknown—talk you out of something you longed to do or try? Creative, courageous living is about forging ahead anyway, onto the uncharted path, even as your nerves rattle.

Especially when they rattle.

Few people understand this better than Margaret Johnson, our chief creative officer. Known for her moxie and Southern drawl, her leadership shorthand is "let's do it." When teams are hesitant or wrestling with a crazy idea, wondering, "How will that happen? How the heck will we pull it off?" Margaret says with complete and casual conviction, "*Let's do it.*"

These three words are deceivingly simple. Yet, they're a bold commitment to action. They inject people with just the right dose of courage and permission they need to go for something, figure it out, and make it happen. And when they do, they uncover new approaches and applications that pave the way for even bigger breakthroughs. Ultimately, what makes creative people creative isn't just their flair for art, words, or song. It's their belief that they can figure it out. Their willingness to risk failure rather than give up.

As Margaret describes it: "It feels like building the plane while you're flying it. You start with an idea that no one knows how you're going to pull off, and you just start building. You're jumping into the darkness, which is scary—but it's also thrilling. You're going to go in some directions that don't work. That's okay—that's part of it. You iterate, and sharpen the good stuff as you go, and if you keep going, you end up somewhere interesting and original, and never perfect. Perfect is boring. Creativity is messy."

I'm inviting you to identify your own fearless firsts. What makes your nerves rattle with excitement? Venture into new spaces and places inspired by the fire of your Life Brief. Play with ideas you've never allowed yourself and let them marinate in your mind. Try something new, even if you don't know where it will lead.

For me, stepping into creative living means challenging myself to think about time differently—to see it as something I can play with, mold, even bend to my will. You know those little valuable pockets of time we can easily spend scrolling social media? I can, and often do, spend hours mindlessly scrolling if I'm not careful.

Armed with the clarity of my Life Brief, on the other hand, I take a different course of action. And I find that I can go further, and feel more alive, in fifteen minutes when I push myself to act than I would with two hours spent on stuff that's meaningless by comparison.

Chip and I recently wrote a Life Brief to "Supercharge Our Health." I had been sitting so much during the pandemic that my chair was branded with my butt print. At first, the idea of committing to a regular workout was daunting—just because I've created a Life Brief around time doesn't mean I don't need to fight for it. My life had become almost entirely sedentary with remote work, and over time, complacency and malaise had set in. My old exercise routines of boot camps and classes were time-consuming—get dressed, ten minutes by car, parking, an hour class, drive home, and shower. There's no way to squeeze that into the morning crunch between school prep, drop off, and my 9:00 a.m. start to the workday. The sheer thought of making that happen demotivated me.

But who says that supercharging my health requires an hour a day of working out? Could I find a way that psyched me up—*and* fit into my limited schedule?

Aha.

Another trait of a creative mindset is finding the shortest path to solving a problem. While we live in a culture of limitless distractions, we also live in the golden age of life hacks, allowing you to bank, work out, or schedule your days with ease.

I discovered an app (actually, several) that delivers fifteen-minute daily workouts, each one different from the day before. I just throw down my yoga mat and press play on the video before I even hit the floor. As small of an act as it is, it kicks off each day with a dose of accomplishment that sets me up to kick ass in other healthy ways. And anytime I feel my motivation slip, I remind myself that supercharging my health is a commitment to act every day, not just when it's convenient.

Experiment, play, be willing to fall down and pick yourself back up again. Creative people are continuously breaking old muscles while building new ones. Courage comes easily when you're lit up by clarity and desire. Even risk feels less risky when desire outweighs and overshadows the fear. Venturing into the unknown isn't as terrifying when you're clear about—and committed to—what you really, really want. A bigger risk is to throw spaghetti at the wall and hope for the best. Even riskier yet is to stand still and go nowhere.

Creativity and courage go hand in hand because when you're stoked by the fires of creativity, the things that scare other people fail to scare you—including the fear of failure. You'll find excitement in the journey of discovery—in letting ideas lead and in iterating new pathways and solutions when your first attempts don't seem to bear fruit.

What idea are you so curious about chasing that you'll be willing to try, fail, and try again?

What dream so lights you up that the idea of not trying is unacceptable?

The Action: Chase Your Goose Bumps

Creative, courageous living is about letting go of limiting thoughts about what is, or is not, possible. It's about tapping into our own "inner aliveness"—that part of us that doesn't readily accept "impossible."

Allow that feeling of aliveness to be your compass and catalyst when you're lost—let it be what propels you out of paralysis. What's tricky, though, is that aliveness shows up differently for each of us. Some of us get butterflies in our stomach. Some of us get goose bumps. Others feel electricity. Still others break out into a nervous sweat. For me, aliveness shows up as a buzzy lightness of being, a sort of natural caffeination. No matter the time of day or night, when an idea strikes my inner bull's-eye, I feel wide awake, senses heightened and lit up from within, unable to let go until I act on it.

A creative mindset harnesses this aliveness and uses it as a propeller for action.

Keep with the Life Brief practice long enough and at a certain point, we start to embody our inner truth in new and surprising ways. Our bodies tell us.

That's why I tell people to chase their goose bumps—or whatever part of your body is speaking to you when a new idea or action presents itself. The next time you get these signals, I encourage you not to shoo them away but to stay with them, as uncomfortable as they may seem at first.

Where and how does aliveness show up in your body?

Mark that feeling. Recognize it, get to know it, and then start to seek it and follow it forward.

Let's return to the "what if . . ." exercise from chapter 15. Generate a new list of "what if . . ." ideas from your Life Brief. Give yourself the freedom and permission to tap into the fullness of your creativity as you make your list. The aim here is not to be realistic or practical. The goal is to be generative. See how many ideas you can come up with, no matter how wild or wacky. In fact, *dare* to be wild and wacky!

- What if _____

  _____

- What if _____

  _____

- What if _____

_____

- What if _____

_____

- What if _____

_____

- What if _____

_____

- What if _____

_____

Once you've emptied your creative reserves, reread your ideas, one at a time. Try each one on and tune in to what emerges emotionally and energetically. Which ideas fire you up? Which ones weigh you down? Which make you chuckle or grin? Which inject you with buzzy aliveness?

Chase the ideas that give you goose bumps (or your own version of them). Visualize them in vivid detail. Brain Dump about them. Allow them to stir you into action, no matter how small, and see what unfolds from there. Be courageous in your commitment to your goose bumps—they will lead you on extraordinary adventures.

CHAPTER 20

TINY ACTIONS
CREATE BIG CHANGE

I'm ready to . . . make change irresistible.

The question: How do I realize my Brief?

The practice: Break it down (don't build it up).

The action: Make It Tiny and Daily.

---

*S*o what now?

What do I do next?

What happens from here?

You're off-roading now, which means there is no right answer to the question "What's next?" Why? Because you're in uncharted territory! You've unearthed desires you may have never known existed. You've committed to living, loving, or working in a way you've never done before.

But while this path you're walking is uniquely yours, you're not alone in this journey. I know what it's like to feel more excited than I've felt in years—and more uncertain than ever about what exactly comes next. I've experienced the same weird up-and-down where one moment I'm thinking, *I'm ready for anything!* and the next I'm thinking, *This is crazy. I'm crazy.* And I've helped more people than I can count through exactly this moment of transition.

And here's what I've witnessed time and time again.

You don't need to work hard to figure out what's next. Your Life Brief will guide and inspire you forward.

People often think that change begins with giant leaps. *Quit my job, break up with my partner, move to a new city.* In my experience, lasting and meaningful change comes more often from a daily flow of micro movements.

If you are ready to activate your Life Brief, focus on tiny, daily actions you can take towards it. Identify one irresistibly small step you can take at a time. When I say irresistible, I mean steps so easy that you simply cannot ignore, excuse, or avoid them. Then, the next day, take another irresistibly small bite out of your Brief. . . . And the next, and the next.

Engage in a practice of incrementalism, not maximalism. Ask yourself, *What can I do that will take less than ten minutes?* Make a list of anything that comes to mind. If you look at what you've written and it still feels hard, think of something even easier—perhaps something you can knock out in just five minutes. How can you break it down even further, until you get to *Duh, why* wouldn't *I do this?*

For my "Supercharge Our Health" Brief, this meant tapping and opening the workout app. When it came to my "Relations, Not Just Solutions" Brief, I might initiate a conversation or send a text asking for guidance. Or if that felt too triggering, heavy, or required too much time, I might read one article about racial equity that day. For "Mad Love," my tiny but mighty act was looking Chip in the eye, leaning over, and showing my appreciation through a momentary kiss.

Sarah is another example of how incrementalism can generate outsized outcomes. Sarah is a writer and editor who had a pattern of setting big, ambitious writing goals that often daunted and pressured her to the point of paralysis. After she wrote a Life Brief to "Reignite [her] Creative Spark," she approached it with *tiny, daily* actions instead of audacious, ambitious ones. The only action she committed to was to "open the document to her novel" each day. Not only was it easy to do, but it was inexcusable *not* to do. This tiny little act changed everything. Some days, when the document was open, Sarah would write one new sentence. Other days, she would write one hundred. But each daily opening of her document kept her connected to her project and her creativity. After two weeks of this practice, Sarah realized she had added over seven thousand words to her novel. More importantly, her writing felt more alive, energized, and joyful. Instead of feeling daunted or paralyzed, Sarah was having fun again.

After Chip and I had aligned around the clarity of our first Life Brief, "Take Our Time," our action steps started out small. We took tiny bites of action during small slivers of time in our messy lives, using our free time for research and brainstorming. I discovered that my excitement about our Brief was drawing me away from news cycles and social feeds. I felt lit up, excited to research communities and schools we might love bit by bit.

While I was nursing or waiting in line for school pickup, I shifted my time organically and automatically, choosing to look at cities with cheaper costs of living instead of scrolling or shopping. I started to play with ideas in my mind. Because I was so juiced up by our Life Brief, all of this was *fun*. And even though my life was just as full, I was able to spend my "in-between time" differently—and Chip was doing the same. The clarity of the Life Brief and our alignment around it nudged us forward in new and unsuspected ways.

We laid this groundwork until we were mentally and emotionally ready to take on more. My first shifts were small, but I followed my curiosity and excitement, checking in constantly about whether an opportunity or idea felt aligned with our Brief and throwing out everything except the most closely connected. There was still plenty to do in between kids, clients, and household needs, but the Brief became an antidote to the false narrative of, "I'm too busy. It's too hard. It's not possible to make this Life Brief real." My attention was awakened, and my drive was ignited by the energy of our Life Brief.

What I want to highlight here is that much of this came easily, naturally, because that's what happens when you achieve clarity. Clarity focuses your attention. Actions follow your attention. You don't have to force or will your way into your Life Brief. For some people, their smallest daily action is to simply start their mornings by rereading their Life Brief, connecting with it, allowing its words to stir and reverberate deep within them.

Paralysis and overwhelm often come from building things up or jumping to outcomes and conclusions. It's all too easy for thoughts to raise the stakes, multiply the hurdles, or complicate the tasks standing between you and your Life Brief. I call this "psyching ourselves into paralysis."

When you feel that overwhelm, "unthink" and move into action. Even if it terrifies you. Overcome the urge to give in or give up—instead think about one very small, one-minute action you can take to reconnect with your practice. Action shatters paralysis—even if the action appears to have no connection to your end game, doing *anything* is more likely to keep you going in the right direction than standing still and doing nothing. When we sit and think for too long, our minds start playing tricks on us, and our doubts give way to spin. They create their own momentum.

The course correction is action.

Change your scenery. A short walk or drive can do the trick. Get moving to break the spell, even if it's just to do some jumping jacks in place. Moving gets us out of our minds so we can find fresh perspectives, return to our situation with new eyes and a beginner's mind—catapult out of the death spiral of doubt. When creatives in advertising get stuck, they get out the front door. They go to a museum or watch a show, and boom. They reward hard pushes with playful pauses. The simple act of zooming out and tuning in to something new and potentially inspiring creates a shift that can break the spin and spark an epiphany.

Another move is to make something—anything. Creation fires up new sensors and redirects our attention and energy into a state of flow that unlocks revelations and epiphanies. When people tinker, experiment, and play, they stumble into ideas they could not have conjured by simply trying to "think harder."

The power of small actions is especially important to remember during moments of transition or crisis.

At the end of 2021, I found myself in burnout mode. I had spent nearly two years in the trenches of pandemic-parenting four kids while helping to lead our agency through the turbulence of seeming financial uncertainty and remote work. In the isolation of quarantine, work crept into every free moment, easily slipping into the new voids of drive time, happy hours, weekend BBQs, and birthday parties. At first the extra productivity seemed natural, welcome even. It felt like I was getting ahead of things, like I was really *nailing it*.

It was only when this heightened degree of productivity became *expected* that I realized we were no longer working from home, we were sleeping at work.

Our kids needed us more than ever, each facing their own unique challenges while navigating the uncertainty. I recall one afternoon, during a client presentation over Zoom, hearing a door slam and shouting in the courtyard. I muted my microphone while acting natural on camera, straining my ears to hear what was unfolding between my husband and son while simultaneously keeping tabs on the tone of our client meeting. Toggling between the worlds of work and family became my new normal. Bringing calm to storms—often more than one at a time—took over my existence and left very little, if any, time for myself. I lost sleep. I woke up racked with anxiety. I experienced, for the first time in my life, mild bouts of depression.

None of this comes as any surprise to working parents. Nor did my situation come close to the degree of crisis so many people faced over these same years. I was aware of my good fortune and privilege even as I wobbled under the weight of our situation. And I was making the choice that mothers everywhere make every day, pandemic or not—prioritizing and putting others ahead of ourselves.

When it came time to write a New Year's Life Brief, I decided to focus it solely on myself. Once again, time thrust forward as the dominating theme. Along with time came the need for solitude, replenishment, and lightness of being—if not outright play. While writing my new Brief came easy—hey, my practice in doing these was paying off!—wondering *if* or *how* it could happen became my biggest block.

I found myself drowning in guilt and limiting stories. *This is too vulnerable of a time to take any breaks. College applications are due. We need to make more headway. I'm only addressing the most pressing and urgent issues at the agency. . . . How will I tackle the truly important work if I take time to myself?*

It didn't stop there. I also started conjuring irrational scenarios that made me feel even more impotent. *The other partners at the agency will devalue me. My employees will feel let down by me. Chip won't be able to maintain the fort of our family if I take some time to myself. My kids will remember me as selfish and self-serving for not just putting work ahead of their needs, but also my own.*

It was as if I had forgotten everything I knew about creative, courageous living.

When I'd finally had enough of my personal pity party, I took the advice I give others when teaching the Life Brief. I zeroed my focus on the next day and thought up the smallest step I could make towards my new Life Brief—"Take Back My Time." I pulled up my calendar and blocked it off at 5:30 p.m. It took less than two minutes and I immediately felt calmer. I promised myself that I would not extend my workday beyond 5:30 unless it was for something truly urgent or important. At first, I scheduled my 5:30 end time for Mondays and Wednesdays. Soon after, I made it my regular workday. I made use of the pre-dinner time for a hike in the hills behind our home or a walk with a friend.

Later, I mustered the guilt-free courage to book a three-day solo weekend with Chip's full support. I rented an inexpensive and rustic tiny house in a rural town a few short hours from our home. I could get home easily if anyone needed me. That getaway revived and replenished me in ways I never expected. Time felt as if it were bending to my every need. I indulged in writing, cooking my favorite meals, taking long walks, and lying under the stars. I even took advantage of the wooden tree swing on the river's edge.

The rewards of these first moves encouraged me to make bigger, more permanent ones. I realized that a big reason I was overworked was that I was taking on too much alone. And in doing so, not only was I drowning in the urgency of immediate demands (and not prioritizing the long game) but I was also robbing talented, impassioned, and well-deserving people under me the ability to step up in their own careers. By elevating people into expanded roles and hiring new leads, I was not only able to create space and time to breathe more deeply but we were able to make important strategic advances at the agency. And the more momentum we generated at work, the more time I was able to carve out for our family and for myself.

Tiny, daily actions break your Life Brief into bite-sized steps that are impossible to excuse or ignore. These actions are the building blocks of momentum, small yet consistent doses of progress and satisfaction.

Let's say your Life Brief involves opening yourself up to new work. How can you hype yourself up instead of psyching yourself out? Don't exhaust yourself by anticipating the drudgery of navigating job boards, getting grilled in interviews, or facing the disappointment of your boss when you resign. That would stop anyone in their tracks!

These thought patterns are not uncommon. We know it isn't healthy but find ourselves doing it anyway.

Break the pattern by taking irresistibly tiny actions.

The Action: Make It Tiny and Daily

Begin a practice of tiny, daily actions that take you closer to your Brief. The operative word here is *daily*. Consistency is key and critical to making real change. You'll get further investing ten minutes a day on your Life Brief than cramming ten hours once in a blue moon. Break things down into tiny, bite-sized pieces and stay present in those steps day by day.

What can you do in ten minutes today?

Write it down.

How do you feel when you look at your ten-minute action on the page?

Does it feel daunting or invigorating? Does it feel easy or hard?

Does it fire up your curiosity—*I wonder what will happen when . . .*?

If you feel daunted, reimagine your action until you arrive at something that stirs a sense of aliveness in you . . . or feels so easy that it would be dumb to ignore.

Is ten minutes overwhelming? Break it down to five.

What can you do in five minutes today?

A Google search?

A quick text?

Initiate a conversation?

A five-minute Brain Dump?

Reread your Brief?

I'm going to update my LinkedIn profile.

I'm going to peek at the open jobs while I'm there.

Oh, that feels hard.

Okay. I am going to just find and read my profile through new eyes.
What can be your irresistible next step?

When you start breaking things down in this way, your Life Brief will feel more manageable and less overwhelming, even as you start to live it. Move forward by doing something ridiculously small. What is the easiest, smallest, most irresistible step you can take today? Whatever it is, DO SOMETHING, even if it's just one tiny thing, each and every day.

CHAPTER 21

MOMENTUM IS YOURS TO MAKE

I'm ready to . . . honor my needs.

The question: How do I stay the course?
The practice: Set yourself up to thrive.
The action: Create Your Peak Conditions.

There may be moments when you feel unmotivated, stuck, and disconnected from your Life Brief. Maybe you're feeling an energy dip or disappointed that change isn't happening faster. If you find yourself skipping your nightly ritual of connecting with your Brief or if even the tiniest actions are starting to feel like a slog, it's a clear sign that it's time to shake things up.

Creating your peak conditions is about setting yourself up to realize your Life Brief—orchestrating your life circumstances so that your Life Brief can manifest. Your peak conditions are any settings, arrangements, or provisions that make you feel invigorated, rejuvenated, and alive. Being keenly aware of your unique peak conditions allows you to consciously set yourself up for momentum.

There are many types of conditions. There's time of day and your personal rhythm. There are the ways you feed and fuel yourself, physically, intellectually, and spiritually. For me, understanding my own ideal conditions meant discovering little things about myself. I've learned that my biggest aha moments strike when I allow myself ten or fifteen added minutes in bed in the morning before rushing to pick up my phone, reading the news, or checking emails. If I allow myself the spaciousness to linger and let my attention wander, my mind starts to steep in its own creativity. I have also discovered that I feel most energized off screens and out in nature, so I have made this an easy go-to step to take when I need to reconnect with myself. And, as much as I hate pre-performance anxiety, I also get fueled by it. The tension of those moments forces a valuable clarity that I use to keep my performance authentic.

I also have conditions I avoid, as we all do. One trigger at work is the feeling that I'm not seeing the whole picture. Because of my long-held fear of outsiderness, I'm prone to anxiety about being excluded and suspicious of hidden agendas. I've found that the fastest remedy and resolution is to puncture my anxiety or suspicions through connection. If I feel isolated, I seek out one-on-one time. If I feel doubt, I reach out to my fans. If I feel misunderstood, I connect with my critics and open a conversation.

Observe your own rhythms and flow to uncover your unique peak conditions. What are the conditions that elevate you? And what are the conditions that deflate you? When do you feel most alive? What's happening around you to fuel that aliveness? How can you stimulate and replicate it? What are the conditions *you* need to thrive?

When you find yourself experiencing "peak" aliveness, pause to take note of what's happening around you. What led you to this moment? What got you to this feeling? What pumps you up even when you're breaking down?

The Action: Create Your Peak Conditions

Let's start by observing, then capturing in writing, the settings and situations that elevate you and set you up for success. While you're at it, you're also likely to notice the situations that drain and suck the life force out of you. Write those things down, too. We cannot orchestrate our peak conditions until we pinpoint what they are—and what stands in their way.

If you're like me, you may find it hard to think up your peak conditions in one sitting. If you're struggling to come up with your optimal conditions from scratch in this moment, I suggest you go back to your collection of Brain Dumps for inspiration. Reread each entry and reflect on the moments when you felt most alive. Unpack those memories to pinpoint what led to or fed your aliveness.

Who or what played a role . . .

- Leading up to the moment?
- During the moment?
- After the moment?

Which of these conditions or circumstances ring true across other memories of aliveness for you? Which can you replicate in the future to set yourself up for more aliveness?

CHAPTER 22

INVITE OTHERS TO PLAY

I'm ready to . . . lean on others.

The question: What do I do when I lose steam?
The practice: Ask for support.
The action: Cast Your Dream Team.

I t's easy to get stuck in thinking that we must do everything alone. The truth is, though, that none of us exists in a vacuum. In advertising, diverse perspectives and creative tension take us to bolder and more interesting places; in our lives, it makes sense that surrounding ourselves with people who light us up, challenge us, and hold us up when we fall strengthens our courage to shoot for the moon.

Think about the people in your life, the ones you turn to when you get wobbly. The ones who make you feel capable and worthy. Who pushes you to see bigger and go further than you think you can? Who nudges you to act on your most potent ideas? Who keeps you going when you are tempted to quit? These people are your Dream Team, the allies that can fuel your forward momentum whenever you're feeling stuck. I'll admit that I cringe a little each time I write the name "Dream Team."

But as cheesy as it sounds, it sticks. I can't unthink it. That's the power of handles—they're sticky. More importantly, the phrase captures the essence of the lesson—surround yourself with people who inspire you, who fuel you, who have your back.

In the last chapter we identified our peak conditions—what did that exploration tell you about who you need as partners and allies? Do you need someone to hold you accountable? Or do you need one of your fans, someone loving and supportive, who's there to say, "You got this. I've seen you do it. Remember this time and that? You got it." Do you need sharp-shooters who remind you to ignore the drainers and naysayers? Do you need people around you who bring out your playfulness—people who spark wild ideas to break you out of your safety zones?

Your Dream Team can be any size that serves you. Maybe one or two people alone can play all the roles you need. Maybe you can identify a few people who already show up for you in this way. Once you're clear about your Dream Team, activate them to become conscious collaborators, supporters, and investors in you and your aliveness. While you don't have to share the specifics of your Life Brief with them, I invite you to tell them the valued role they play in your life and your desire to enlist them as a crucial part of your Life Brief journey.

Each time you notice one of your thought enemies rearing its ugly head, you'll know who to turn to. Each time you find yourself in need of a nudge or even a shove, you'll know who will provide it. Have these people on speed dial, always at the ready. We are not alone in change, and we have to call in support when we need it.

The Action: Cast Your Dream Team

Make a cast list. Surround yourself with people who see, honor, support, and deepen your truth . . . instead of those who try to manage, control, doubt, or silence it. Who will challenge you and support you in living your Brief?

1. **Anchor:** Who helps you stay true to who you are?
2. **Believer:** Who makes you feel capable and worthy?
3. **Visionary:** Who pushes you to see bigger and go further than you think you can?
4. **Firestarter:** Who nudges you to act on your most potent ideas?
5. **Fuel:** Who keeps you going when you want to quit?
6. **Vault:** Who guards your secrets and catches you when you fall apart, free from judgment?
7. **Truthteller:** Who gifts you the truth in ways that propel you forward?

Choose one person from your Dream Team and share your Life Brief with them. Activate them by telling them their role in your life and invite them to lean into it.

CHAPTER 23

LIFE IS A DANCE

I'm ready to . . . let go of control.

The question: How do I get others to change?
The practice: Invite change with your actions.
The action: Shift from *What You Want* to *How You Want.*

There's always someone at my retreats or workshops who asks, "Can I Life Brief my boss?" or "When do I get to Life Brief my kids?," "How do I Life Brief my best friend or partner?" Much as we might like the answers are *no, never,* and *don't even think about it*! —you cannot "Life Brief" someone else. But once our Life Briefs are written, we get to shift how we dance with the people in our lives. When we shift how *we* show up, we invite the dance partners in our lives to dance differently, too. That's how change happens.

We aren't in control of everything, but we *do* control our own choices and actions. And each time you make a move, you invite others to react and respond. Think of your life as a dance, and your Life Brief as an instruction manual for how to dance to your own favorite beat—and to move in rhythm with the world around you.

The first question of the Life Brief practice was, *What do you want?* For many of us, our immediate answers were tangible, external desires—*I want to be with this person. I want to earn this salary. I want to land this job. I want this house—*.

The next layer of Life Briefing takes you to *how you want*—how you want to feel, how you want to experience, or how you want to act. When we turn our attention to *how we want to be, feel, or experience our lives—*change often emerges immediately, unlocking surprising new doorways in our lives. *How you want* is a turn to accountability, a shift from desire to agency, seeing that *you* are the key to change in your life. When you get clear about how you want to show up differently—love differently, work differently, lead differently, nourish yourself or others differently—you invite everyone and everything in your life to follow your lead.

Well into my adult life, I continued to grapple with my relationship with my dad, the impact it had on my life as a child and an adult. Our dance was not at all fluid; it had been rocky, uncertain, and on too many occasions, volatile. The thought of his death loomed over me for decades. Countless threats of dying. So many that it became the wallpaper of my childhood.

His unpredictable volatility continued to live on the edges of my mind long into adulthood. Memories of blowups and meltdowns dominate my recollections, vivid and visceral. Sitting frozen, barely breathing, across the kitchen table, praying for him to tire of his rants and threats. Driving home from family gatherings, swerving across the freeway, him yelling, laying on the horn, while my brother and I lay low in the back seat. I can't shake the feeling of those thin-waisted seat belts, the force of his rage as it spewed out at nearby drivers. Moments like these were etched into my being, as was my longing for connection or closure. Eventually, the distance between us grew. I escaped by racing to build a life of my own. Yet his shadow followed me. It fueled my ambition and defiant independence; it strengthened and solidified my resolve to parent with care and compassion. But I never stopped longing to mend our past.

By the end of his life, his depression and mental health issues had become so severe that he neglected every single aspect of his physical health. He stayed in his bedroom, the heat turned up like a sauna, smoking and sleeping throughout each passing day. He refused to leave the house except for visits to the doctor. When we visited him, he would come out for short periods of time before retreating again into his bedroom. At a certain point, mobility became an issue, and after we moved to Portland, we'd resigned ourselves to spending holidays without him.

Then one year, a week before Christmas, he called and asked if he could fly to Portland for the holiday. I was elated and daunted. It had been so long since the last time everyone was together. But how would we make it happen? He was living in a residential care facility, incontinent and unable to walk, much less travel on his own. He still had unexpected, and at times physical, outbursts when he disagreed with his care. And my mom wasn't able to accompany him. In an act of incredible grace, my dear friend Cyndi offered to help transport and accompany him to the airport.

On Christmas Day I remember wandering around the house, from room to room. Everyone was there, our entire family together, three full generations. The fire was roaring, and there was my dad sitting in his wheelchair, amidst the bustle—kids, games, and wrapping paper everywhere. As I silently soaked up the scene, I knew this would be the last time we would all be together. My father must have felt it, too, because the next morning at breakfast, he told me, "I don't want to go back to LA. I want to stay here."

We were raising four young kids and I was spending two days each week in our San Francisco office. Chip was already working hard to stay on top of our kids' needs, I couldn't ask him to also take on the full-time care my Dad required. But even though I knew all of that to be true, it didn't make telling him any less wrenching.

"I'm sorry, Daddy," I said. "As much as I want to, we can't . . ."

On the drive home from the airport, tears pouring down my face, I was gripped by guilt and the fear that my dad's death would come without a chance to reconcile our relationship. I longed to let my father know that I saw his struggle and pain, his sacrifices and suffering, all in service of providing us with new beginnings. I desperately longed for him to feel the fullness of my love, to make up for my years of anger, resentment, and later, absence.

That night, I wrote a Life Brief centered in *forgiveness*. That single word was the handle for it. In it I wrote three simple points.

- I'm ready to name the struggle.
- I'm ready to acknowledge the pains.
- I'm ready to surrender to forgiveness.

After writing the Life Brief, I wondered if and how I would ever turn my longing into action. Six months later, I got my chance.

I was preparing for a new business pitch when I saw the text from my mom. *Dad's in the hospital. The doctor wants to speak to you and your brother.* I knew what was coming before the doctor said a word. I panicked and prayed for more time, even though I had no clue as to what I would do with it. I jumped on a flight to LA.

For so much of my life, my father was a terrifying presence. But during the last week of his life, it was he who was terrified. Though he could no longer speak, I could see the fear alert in his eyes. He was intent on holding to life, even as his body began its own course of shutting down.

The doctor came into the room and informed us that it was time to remove the supplemental oxygen machine. There was nothing more the medical team could do to change the course of the inevitable. My dad, still conscious, shook his head, eyes pleading to be heard. My brother and I defended his wishes and refused the removal of the respirator. When the medical team left the room, we gathered as a family around my father's bed.

I inhaled deeply and centered myself. I looked into his eyes and said with the full force of my care and conviction, "Daddy, we love you. Thank you for the sacrifices you made to raise us, bring us to this country, give us the chance to make something of ourselves." His eyes softened. Then, to my surprise, my mother leaned over and whispered into his ear, "Thank you, Charles. You have been a good husband, father, and provider. You have given us a good life."

My mom's final words to my dad were ones I never imagined hearing. She reached out to him with a love and tenderness I could not recall in the recesses of my memories. My brother followed with his love and reassurance. After a long pause, I sensed my father's fear rise again.

Looking steadily and deeply into his eyes I said, "It's all right, Dad, you can let go now. There is nothing to be afraid of. I promise."

He looked back at me, closed his eyes, and reopened them with a nod. I saw his acceptance, his permission, his peace. It was only then that my brother reached over, gently lifting Dad's head to remove the ventilator mask.

I spent the night in his room, that last night, on the tiny foldout armchair. The sounds of his labored breathing provided a strange sense of reassurance and comfort.

We spent those final days in the hospital together as a family. An entire lifetime showed up and mended in one week of closure. And over the course of those days, I witnessed moments I thought I'd never see or experience. It was just the four of us in that hospital room, back to the core of our family. Just us for four beautiful days.

The hardest relationship in my life came together in its final days. Only when I was able to get clear that I was ready for true forgiveness was I finally able to accept my dad's pain as his pain and accept him for the life that he had lived. It allowed me to dance differently in those final days. Instead of being the helpless, resistant, regretful child, I was able to show up as his guide. I was able to be his voice, defend his will and wishes from the hospital's protocols. I was able to be a facilitator for my family, for my mother, and through my own actions, invite her to dance differently for him and for all of us. And finally, I was able to show up and be his bridge to peace and offer him the strength to let go.

I came to the end of a lifetime of rocky roads with my father and found what I had longed for—forgiveness. What surprised me in those moments was the realization that I had forgiven him years before. What I had actually been seeking—and what I finally found—was forgiveness for myself.

In showing up with the fullness of my presence, giving voice to his desires, and offering him the peace and permission to let go, I was able to mend my own heart. I had spent most of my life running from him, holding on to dark images of his and our past. It wasn't until that final year of his life that I was able to apply my own strength and wisdom to finding peace with my memories and with my father. I had developed an ability to care for myself and give to myself what I had always longed to receive from him.

I wouldn't have been able to show up in any of those ways if I had not first done the work to examine the complexity that my father's legacy had left on my life starting at such an early age. My practice with Life Briefing the different areas of my life gave me the courage to face this one. And because of that, my Forgiveness Brief allowed me to shift our roles and to give him the gift of acceptance—something I longed to receive from him, only to realize that I had to give it first.

The lesson I learned from that final week with my dad is that the course of every relationship begins with *me*. My choices determine the dance that ultimately unfolds. While we cannot control the people, situations, or circumstances around us, we are always in control of our own moves.

No one understands this wisdom more than my friend Molly. When I met her some twenty years ago, she had already experienced a lifetime of loss. Her father died by suicide late in her teens, and not long after we met, she lost a dear friend to a horrific homicide. She has lost other friends to stroke, cancer, and COVID. Most recently, her brother took his own life.

And yet despite that, Molly is an effervescent person who seems to walk through life with wonder and ease. She speaks openly about the people she's lost and her experiences with death. During a weekend together, I asked her whether people view her as someone in denial.

"Do people think that you avoid grief?"

"Oh yeah," she responded. "I don't grieve the same way as other people. Which means I also don't grieve in the ways some people expect me to grieve. But I do grieve. I grieve by celebrating the roles people I've lost played in my life. I celebrate by making their gifts my own. I adopt them and reflect them back out to the world."

Some people might describe Molly's life as one paved with tragedy, but she chooses to frame it differently. She doesn't buy into social rules around grief or societal expectations for navigating separation. She thinks, *Wait a second. I can do this my way. I have that choice.*

We all have that choice. And it's always available. Even in the bleakest of moments, we can choose how we experience our circumstances and relationships—with another person, with ourselves, or with anything near and dear to us.

The Action: Shift from *What You Want*
to *How You Want*

You are the key to unlocking change in your life. The fastest path there is to ask *how you want* questions instead of *what you want* questions. When you get clear about how you want to shift—how you want to show up differently in your relationship, at work, or for yourself—everything opens up.

When we aim our attention at *how we want* to be, feel, and behave differently, we shift into accountability and agency for our own choices. This shift in mindset invites a shift in actions—and *that* invites *everyone and everything* around us to shift, catapulting us towards real and immediate change.

- How do you want to be in your most important relationships, in your work, and for yourself?
- How do you want to feel?
- How do you want to show up for yourself and for others?
- How do you want to love?
- How do you want to receive?
- How do you want to serve?

In what ways are you ready to dance differently?

CHAPTER 24

MOURN THE TRANSITION

I'm ready to . . . step into change.

The question: How do I overcome my resistance?

The practice: Make space for mourning.

The action: Honor What Was.

W*hat if nothing's happening? Was I a dummy for believing any of this? Where is the change?*

Where is my serendipity?

Because I'm not seeing it.

Some Life Briefs take longer than others to manifest. Others don't have a finish line or conclusion.

We can't see into the unknown nor plan for the unpredictable. Life happens.

Change unfolds in mysterious ways and at its own pace.

Yet the Life Brief keeps our view on the horizon, on what lights us up. The Brief is our anchor to *what matters most*, even as the seas toss our boat and threaten to shake it off course.

In the meantime, we have responsibilities and housekeeping that need to be met and tackled. And there's something beautiful about the moments between the miracles that I've come to accept—even cherish.

A few years ago, I lost my dear friend Christopher to cancer. Not long before he passed, while he was still lucid and had clarity of mind, we spent an evening in his art studio, which he'd converted from his garage. I was updating him about the Life Brief, and Chris was beaming with excitement about its growing momentum. "You know, Bonnie," he said, "I love the Life Brief. But you have to let people know that after they get clear about what they want, they still have to show up for the housekeeping. There's always going to be housekeeping."

I listened intently as he continued, "I have stage 4 cancer. I am going to die, but I still have to get up, make my bed, take my boy to school, do the dishes, make sure the space around us is healthy for our kids. Even with stage 4 cancer, I don't get a hall pass. You gotta keep your eyes on the horizon. Know what you want and what matters while making it a part of how you show up for your duties."

His point in that moment was that, even in the face of life-altering change, there were responsibilities for him to honor, commitments that grounded him as he and his family prepared for what the future held.

It's true that uncertainty and unknowing can resurface or trigger doubt. Doubt turns into resistance, towards yourself and your Brief. And resistance pulls us back to the safety of the familiar, protecting us from change and the dangers of disappointment.

It can be tempting to retreat from your Life Brief, especially when you are on the brink of choosing to make a big change or shift. I have come to the edges of giving up on many Life Briefs. I have memories seared into my mind of despairing parenting moments when I thought our Brief had damaged and distanced our kids, only to have them come in closer. There have been nights I found myself racked with doubt, questioning my relation-centered Work Brief, just before the turnaround of a tricky employee situation. Each time this happens, I remind myself that tension is where the fruit is. Instead of overthinking, let's embrace that what we want is going to lead us somewhere different than we've ever been before.

Change itself can be daunting. It can trigger deep fears and intensify agitation. *What if this isn't what I want? What if I'm wrong? What if I regret going for it?* When Chip and I were getting ready to follow our first Life Brief all the way to Portland, the saying "better the devil you know than the devil you don't" came front and center for us—it felt like we were actively testing whether that saying was true. *Maybe we aren't as frustrated as we originally thought,* we wondered. *Maybe we're being dramatic.*

Things were moving forward quickly, and the pressure to commit was mounting; we had to be intentional about going for what we wanted if we wanted to truly live our Life Brief.

As our move to Portland got closer, everything in our brains screamed, *It's real, it's real, it's real.* With everything at stake and the train taking off at speed, everything you love about your life *as it is* comes sharply and vividly into focus. We began to second-guess everything. *Do we want to throw everything against the wall and change our lives? What if it's not all that we thought it would be? How badly do we want this Life Brief? Can't we create our Life Brief right where we were? Surely, we don't have to make such a drastic move.*

After we signed the lease for the house, Chip and I broke out in heated debate in front of friends and family. I made a critical comment about our life in California. In defense, Chip accused me of rejecting our current town, the town we'd invested in for so many years.

"I don't know that I want to move," he said, and I was plunged deeper into doubt.

We were having a meltdown of resistance. We had committed to having time and space for what mattered most—carving our own road—yet we found ourselves face-to-face with the fears of acting on that commitment.

In hindsight, I now recognize our resistance as a need for mourning. Before we could leap into what was next, we needed to make space to mourn what was. We had invested energy, heart, and time into our current town. We had wonderful friends and a community we believed in. And though I was feeling terrible burnout, I was worried about whether my transition to remote work would come with unexpected or unintended hardship. We were leaping towards a life that *sounded* good—that literally looked like what we'd wanted on paper—but what if we were fooling ourselves?

We are most vulnerable during moments of transition. Yet change presents an opportunity to reflect on and release our past. Each time we open a new chapter, sadness will find us, wearing different faces, delivered in different forms. Being present with it and creating space for it allows for its eventual release. Change is hardest to embrace when the loss of our past is palpable, and the payoffs are not yet in sight.

I call it creative, courageous living. Others call it a leap of faith.

But it's important to call out that the Life Brief isn't about blind confidence. Creative, courageous living is the ability to act, leap, or keep moving forward, even when confidence is nowhere to be found.

Remember, the Life Brief is not a plan, it's a practice. The only confidence we need is confidence in our ability to adjust and grow based on our experiences. Chip and I have come to recognize when our fears are talking and holding us back. In noticing these patterns, we have also uncovered our own methods of confronting and overcoming them.

We chose to move forward with our Brief rather than to give in to the doubts and sadness that came with our move. We had made ourselves a promise. Do not fear moving. Do not fear lack of money. Those promises were also a part of our Brief. So we took the leap.

That "leap" turned into a glorious six-year chapter of our lives. Without that tearstained Life Brief I would have never dared to imagine such an opportunity, much less let it in. I would have told myself no or talked myself out of it. We not only declared our desire for change but we acted on it while still tending to the housekeeping of our lives . . . until our Brief became our reality.

Leaping is now a central part of my Life Brief practice.

The Action: Honor What Was

Each time we open a new chapter, we must close the previous one. Yet sometimes we are running so fast into what's next that we overlook the magnitude of honoring what was. We underestimate the potency of saying "thank you" or the power of ritualizing closure.

What are tangible ways you can show or share your appreciation for what has been? Who or what can you bring in to support you? Here are some of the rituals I and other Life Briefers have used in moments of mourning. Let these inspire you, or tap into your own meaningful way of acknowledging your appreciation for what was.

- Write a letter of thanks to what you are leaving behind.
- Share memories and stories.
- Invite new ways to stay connected to what you treasured, as you leap into what's next.

Perhaps the easiest and healthiest way to make space for mourning is to simply allow yourself to feel it—to soak in the sadness when it arrives. Don't stuff or shoo it away. Instead, welcome and embrace it. Allow yourself to feel it in full without the fear that it will derail your plans.

As with many of the practices throughout this book, allow your feelings to be your guide. When discomfort appears or resistance emerges, meet it with curiosity and name what shows up. Take note of your emotions in writing. Ask yourself:

- What am I feeling? Name it. Is it fear, sadness, loss, or something else?
- What is it calling my attention to? What does it need in this moment?
- How can I acknowledge or honor it without denying or rejecting it?

CHAPTER 25

YOUR BRIEF EVOLVES WITH YOU

I'm ready to . . . keep the practice alive.

The question: What if what I want changes?
The practice: Keep iterating.
The action: Revisit Your Brief.

Your Life Brief is a living document, not a destination. It's a practice that evolves as you evolve. I have written Life Briefs for almost every aspect of my life—my relationships, my career, for myself, and for the causes that matter most to me. As you continue the practice of the Life Brief, you'll find it helpful to come back to your Briefs with a fresh perspective.

The practice of writing a Life Brief is a continuous and more enthusiastic engagement with your path than traditional goal setting. Each time I revisit one that I've written in the past, simply reading it becomes an invitation to refine and rewrite. Like life itself, the Life Brief is a series of recommitments.

When Regan began her Life Brief practice, she wasn't ready to shine light on the depth of her inner turbulence. She started by meeting herself where she was ready—her career and her outer life. Yet, even as she took leaps forward in landing a new job and moving to a new city, she allowed her curiosity to continue to stir up other paths to change. *Is my relationship with alcohol different from other people's? Could I talk to someone about it?* Regan acted on these questions in small and large ways, over time. Her continued practice of leading with curiosity, allowing her self-inquiry to guide her actions, unlocked the uncomfortable truths that ultimately propelled her towards a new life.

Each person's journey unfolds differently, so each Life Brief practice takes on its own twists and turns. Because you are off-roading, charting your unique course, it's impossible to predict where yours will go. And while that might sound daunting, it can also be thrilling.

I met a man named Samuel in one of my workshops who came right out of the gate declaring, "I know exactly what I want. I want to be a recording artist, actor, and author. I want to win such and such awards." Samuel was so clear that he could even name the specific dollar amount he wanted in the bank. He had been working for years at becoming a renowned performer, touring the country doing shows for growing numbers of people, and his idea of what he was working towards in life was very "outer"-centric.

But as we went through the steps of the Life Brief, he began to question his industry—and the impact it was having on his inner world. Rather than focusing on his long-held image of fame and success, he tuned in to feelings bubbling up that he realized he'd been suppressing for years. The cutthroat nature of the industry had been getting to him, and his time on the road had taken him away from his family in a way that he regretted.

A couple of years after that workshop, Sam shared that after engaging with his Life Brief, he began to switch gears. He started dedicating more time to his boys, realizing that there was a richness to being there for them that he didn't feel onstage. As Sam's Life Brief evolved, as he revisited and reconsidered it, sharpening it time and again, he found himself increasingly drawn towards his family—the joys of guiding and coaching his boys allowed him to reconnect with the boy deep within himself. Through the revision practice, Sam moved from *I want fame* to *I want fulfillment.*

Sam's story is a good example of the journey of re-envisioning. His first Brief was centered in classic achiever ambitions—becoming a successful performer and published author. He'd invested years of work into honing and perfecting his craft, but as he dove into the earliest parts of his Life Brief, he began to question the emotional resonance of his long-expressed desires. The further he walked the performance path, the less it resonated with him. The more heat he felt around his career, the less he found that he wanted it.

As he evolved his Brief, Sam faced, wrestled with and eventually let go of expectations he carried about "success" while awakening to the growing sense of wealth within him. With time, the words he'd originally written in his Brief rang less and less true to him. It was tough to acknowledge that he'd been chasing a dream that didn't align with his values. He sensed that even if he achieved the success he first visualized, it would not exhilarate and stimulate him as he'd initially imagined. Realizing this allowed him to refocus his time on what *did* fill his life with meaning.

This is a common journey with the Life Brief, and one that I have traveled myself. I, too, have flirted with, questioned, then challenged and discarded the "rules of the rat race." This is what it means to *carve our own path*. I have discovered that the more I ask myself, *What do I want?* the less I find myself wanting societal markers of success. It could be because as I look around, I see that the life I have created is the life I imagined—a life of meaningful reward that unfolds without the rigidity of traditional "plans." My Brief gives me the clarity to see and appreciate how the things I have worked for are showing up in my life.

Yet, I suspect that there is also something deeper at play. My response to *What do I want?* over the years has less and less to do with anything tangible or external. It has more to do with how I experience people, serve my loved ones as well as a greater good while nourishing myself. And yes, while I have achieved classic, material success in the eyes of many . . . it has been a by-product, not the center, of my Life Briefs.

- Take our time.
- Be rich in relationship.
- Rekindle mad love.
- Walk a path of fulfillment, not just achievement.
- Forgive.

These are just a few of the Life Briefs I have written over a decade. And while each of their messages is timeless—as relevant today as when I wrote them—there have been others that I have outgrown, like "Earned Abundance" or "Attract Win after Win."

My Life Briefs have deepened over the years, my longings more centered in *how* I want to be, show up, and serve than *what* I want to have or achieve; my desires more focused on what I want to give than what I want to get. But this is me, a focus group of one. The beauty of the Life Brief practice is that there is no right or wrong way to do it. You are the key to making your Life Brief uniquely yours.

The Action: Revisit Your Brief

Over the years I have met people who revisit their Brief daily and others who do it before a big milestone, like a birthday or anniversary. Chip and I have an annual ritual that takes place on the night of New Year's Day. We'll make a fire, get cozy, and reread our last shared Brief while reimagining our next. I reread my Briefs whenever I find myself confused, frustrated, or at a tricky crossroads. And sometimes, I randomly reread a Life Brief just because.

The reason writing is at the heart of this practice is because writing allows us to be in relationship with our deepest desires and our truth. When we look at our words on the page, we immediately and automatically feel something. That feeling acts as our guide for what to do next. If that feeling is, "Fuck YES!" then you know your Brief still captures what you really, really want in a part of your life that matters most. If your feeling is any version of "Hmm..." or "Huh?" or "Yeah, but..." then it's time that you step into your beginner's mind and let your curiosity uncover the next iteration of your Brief.

Each time you revisit your Life Brief, check in with yourself:

1. First, find your quiet and drop into your "knowing."
2. What do you feel when you read your Brief?
3. Where can your Life Brief be even more honest or truer to what calls to you?
4. What can you add, cut, or rephrase to get to that "Fuck yes!" feeling?

CONCLUSION

ALL THE TIME IN THE WORLD

Life is short.

We have a limited amount of time to live as fully as we can—to show up honestly, love freely and fiercely, serve ourselves and those around us. Your Life Brief is your reminder to live this fleeting and precious life without regrets.

If you take one thing away from the Life Brief practice, it's that "no regrets living" is always available to you, anytime you want it. No matter how rough things get, you always have the choice to drop out of chaos, tune in to yourself, and ask penetrating questions to help bring you closer to your truth. These are the strategies that can help cut through messiness and open a gateway to clarity, creativity, and courageous action.

But in order to act from that place of truth, you must first get curious.

Early on in our marriage, Chip and I were walking down the street, newlyweds just having a casual conversation, when the talk suddenly got more serious. Holding hands, we crossed Valencia Street in the Mission District of San Francisco where we lived. He turned to me and said, "I married you to spend a lifetime with you, and that's my priority. If we aren't meant to have kids, that's completely fine with me. What do you want?"

In that moment, my answer was clear. I, too, was accepting of not having children if that was not meant to be our path. But I also knew that I was curious enough about parenting to give that curiosity my attention.

I knew that if I did not at least *explore* my curiosity that I would come to the end of life feeling as if I were maybe missing something.

That's what "no regrets living" means to me. My thought in that moment wasn't, *I have to have children.* It was, *I want to make myself available to every experience my curiosity wants to taste. Because at the end of this lifetime, I don't want to look back and wonder why I didn't go for it.*

I share this story not because I think you should pursue parenthood, or any other metric that is not wholly your own. My hope for you is that you will follow your curiosity towards any destination that interests you, even if it is unexpected, unconventional, or a little scary. A Life Briefer named Beth recently shared an experience with me that reminded me of my own—not because of the choice she made, but because of the deep inner knowing at the heart of her decision. A man she'd just begun seeing shared that he wanted kids and asked if she felt the same. Though the relationship was new, she really liked him. And so, she shocked herself when she didn't hesitate or try to sugarcoat her words—nope, kids weren't for her.

She knew her curiosity was pulling her to live a different kind of life than the one he wanted. She's never regretted the choice, and she and the man remain friends. When Beth sees photos of his growing family on social media, she feels happiness for them—and equally happy for her own life with her new partner, no kids, and the most spoiled poodle on the East Coast.

Every day, I come across stories like Beth's—of people declaring what they want out of life and how they want to show up for it. And each day, I get to reap the rewards of my own Life Brief practice.

Now that you are walking the path of the Life Brief, how will you clearly and courageously create a life that is uniquely your own? What shifts are you ready to make in the parts of your life that matter most? No, not in dramatic, sweeping ways, but through tiny, daily bite-sized steps that open you up to surprise and serendipity?

Are you willing to honor your curiosity and start asking yourself the questions that scare you? Questions like, What do *you* want? What do you long for? What beckons you?

And as importantly . . . *How* do you want? *How* do you want to feel, experience, show up, and serve?

We are a society fixated on happiness. But happiness isn't something you can hack, innovate, or fast-track. It's also not a continuous state of play or positivity. It does not rise in correlation to an increase in income, status, likes, shares, or followers. Instead, happiness lies in connecting and relating to others through your truth—your innermost voice—even when it goes against conventional wisdom and the status quo. Happiness is an outcome, or maybe a reward, of doing the important and necessary work on ourselves and for our most meaningful relationships.

Perhaps this is what has been eluding so many of us for so long. Maybe we've been taught there's a finish line when it comes to our career goals and relationships—and on the other side is the prize of a good life. But high-fulfillment people are not necessarily the high-achieving people we read about in news headlines. That's because they're not singularly focused on one dimension or "marriage" of life. Instead, they weave together all the strands of their lives into a rich tapestry. They've learned to live inside-out.

The Life Brief invites you to do the same.

You can author your life, or you can be passive to it. You can react to your circumstances, or you can create the conditions that set you up for aliveness. You can try to fit within someone else's program, or create a self-directed life guided by your own callings, propelled by personal agency. This choice is always available. The invitation is evergreen, yours for the taking.

You might feel unsteady at first, but your intuition will strengthen, deepen, and grow. You will move differently through your world. And the world will dance differently with you. You might step, stride, or leap. Regardless of your pace, the clarity of the Life Brief is the shortest distance between you and the change you long for.

When you release yourself from self-doubt and limiting narratives, you make space to see opportunities you would have otherwise over-looked. Changing your story changes your life.

Life is brief. Make it meaningful. Make it yours.

ACKNOWLEDGMENTS

Gratitude. It's overused yet underexpressed.

This is one place where I refuse to be brief.

Chip, Zig, Ila, Ruby, and Mabel, my life would be empty and my briefs would be blank without each of you. Chip, you are the strongest man I know. You are heart and soul before ego. I thank the universe every day for our union. Kids, I hope you read this book someday. And if you do, may it serve you in the days when I can't be by your side. May it anchor you in what matters most—family. We are better together. With our hearts in the right place, we will not go wrong.

Mom, Dad, and Ken, thank you for life itself. None of this would exist without you. Thank you to my cousins, aunties, uncles, grandparents, and ancestors. I am proud to be an extension of you. Yoojin, Yuna, Joe, Kathy, and Karen, thank you for your ongoing love and support.

This book would not exist without my book family. Rachel Neumann, what can I say? You are an intoxicating mix of marvel, magic, and moxie. Thank you for betting on me and *The Life Brief* after just one breakfast. Thank you for telling me that authors don't have to be great writers, but they do need to have something important to say. That alone gave me the courage to say yes! Thank you for helping me see that birthing a book is indeed a collaborative act. It's in that collaboration that I discovered the writer within me.

Leah Miller and Richard Rhorer, thank you for seeing and seizing the potential of *The Life Brief* and making it one of the founding titles for Simon Element. I will forever relish and relive the magic of our first meeting along with the jaw-dropping shock of your offer twenty-four hours later. It still makes me think, *Holy fuck, did that really happen?!*

Leah, you are a master class in the art of creative feedback. I felt seen and safe in every step of your care. Thank you for giving clear, artful, and actionable direction (e.g., "lead a blind horse to water") without ever asking to alter my vision, voice, or content . . . not one single time. I dream that this is just the beginning between us.

Felice Laverne and Sarah Rainone, thank you for uncovering and unlocking my voice, and drafting it into words on the page. Felice, you have set the standard for joyful collaboration. You are excellence embodied— your words, your calm, and your gentle, guiding hand were salves in the trenches. You are method in the messiness, grace under pressure, and through it all, my wayfinder. Sarah, thank you for helping to bring it all home and across the finish. You were the polish that made everything shine and sing. Thank you for squeezing out more stories and word count when all I insisted on was brevity. We would still be in draft form if it wasn't for you.

Thank you, Doug Abrams and Lara Love Hardin, for saying yes after that first meeting in Santa Cruz. You were clear that there was a limit to the number of books in your future. I'm thrilled this one nudged its way into your library. Thank you to Ty Love and the teams at Idea Architects, Simon Element, and Hilsinger-Mendelson. It takes a village to publish a book, and I thank each of you for giving this one your attention, care, energy, and time.

Thank you to my GS&P family for being my home and home base for the arc of my career. Thank you for steeping me in the misfit magic of creativity and for encouraging me to express myself as a leader and strategist in ways that were true to me yet unconventional for our industry. Thank you for fueling the fire of *The Life Brief* from its very start. It takes a uniquely special kind of company to not only embrace but encourage a passion project others would see as a threat or distraction. Thank you for putting people and ideas first and proving that the creative spirit and human spirit can coincide to create triple wins. Rich and Jeff, thank you for creating this one-of-a-kind sandbox and inviting me to play in it. Lester, Margaret, and Christine, it has been a privilege learning from and leading alongside each of you—breaking barriers, opening doors, and supporting each other through thick and thin. Lester, you are both a wise Buddha and a force of nature. Thank you for always encouraging me to do me. Margaret, you are a groundbreaking, ceiling-busting cowgirl. Thank you for lifting as you rise. Christine, thank you for being a beacon of excellence, setting the bar, and pushing boulders up mountains. Derek, thank you for championing my potential, believing in me when I didn't believe in myself, and betting on me when it went against the grain of traditional business logic. Dr. Jennifer Gomes, thank you for your deep well of wisdom and unyielding determination to change the game in service of everyone. Jill, thank you for being a first believer. The warmth of seeing you and Andy Grayson sitting side-by-side in the audience at the very first workshop emboldened me to share my stories and step into the unknown. Babes, you called it from the jump. Brian, thank you for being my first editor—that *Campaign* article would not have gone viral without your guiding hand. David, thank you for literally investing in me and the Life Brief over the years. You have been a quiet pillar of "knowing" in times of need. Deep gratitude to Shirin and Natasha. It would've been damn near impossible to dance between my non-negotiables (family, the agency, and this book) without you.

My heart goes out in full to those who trusted me to tell their stories. Your honesty, vulnerability, bravery, and breakthroughs color the pages of this book, illuminating the way forward for every reader. You are living examples of creative, courageous living, and proof that it comes in many shapes and sizes.

Many exercises in this book were shared by generous minds and open hearts. Diane Tompkins, Mari Pilar Cortizo, Pam Scott, Sarah Pemberton, Sarah Rainone, and Stephanie Phillips, thank you for expanding *The Life Brief*'s toolbox.

To my endorsers, Adam Morgan, Dave Evans, Deepak Chopra, Dr. James Doty, Elle Harrison, Eric Ryan, Esther Wojcicki, Eve Rodsky, Jason Harris, Jeff Goodby, Kat Gordon, Kiki Koroshetz, Lori Gottlieb, Mick Ebeling, and Valentine Giraud, thank you for betting on me and backing this book when it was nothing more than a skinny proposal. The weight of your words gave everyone confidence in its power and potential.

To the game changers who altered the trajectory of *The Life Brief* and threw it into hyperdrive: Meredith Vellines, your fierce, dogged persistence has been a constant stream of jet fuel for *The Life Brief* since its start. Thank you for pushing and prodding me to get this idea and practice beyond the walls of GS&P and into the world. Without you, TLB would not have sailed from agency talk to industry workshop to self-published workbook and beyond. Gabriella Dishotsky, thank you for creating Boost and giving *The Life Brief* its debut. Sarah Pemberton, thank you for being a forever friend and founding fan; teacher and collaborator; seer and magic maker. Kat Gordon, thank you for giving *The Life Brief* wings on its first big stage. Thank you for saying yes to supporting it every step of the way from Detroit to NYC to Costa Rica and the 3% Accelerator. Olivia and Dylan Mullen, thank you for being the keys to the Goop community, catapulting *The Life Brief* beyond the walls of business. Marielle Lorenz, thank you for being the open heart that opens doors. You made *THE* introduction that unlocked and changed everything. I am eternally grateful.

Every idea has an origin story. *The Life Brief* would not be what it is without its predecessor, Project Juice. Mari, you were the *first*—partner, friend, co-creator—on this juicy journey. Emily Collins, Ashley Slack, Dion and Amy Lim, Annie Byrne, Clara, Linda Bradford, Lotta Alsen, and the women of Camp Change, thank you for planting the seeds. We were ahead of our time.

As *The Life Brief* grew from small stages to bigger ones, from workbook to website to newsletter to full-fledged book, it needed more attention than I could give on my own. A tremendous thank-you to the cocreators and collaborators who donated their time and talents to giving *The Life Brief*, well, life: Alesha Hanson, Archetype, Chris Peel, Dessa Brennan, Emily Collins, Jen Hedrick, Kate Phillips, Katy Hill, Noah Dasho, Rachael Stamps, Sarah Pemberton, Sydney Faulkerson, Todd King, Tyler Young, Will Hung.

Thank you to the beacons and believers who took *The Life Brief* to new stages and spaces: *Ad Age*; Alicia Mowder; Allison Kent Smith at Giide; Andy Grayson; Amy Parker and Gina Pell of The What Alliance; Anne Faricy; Annie Morita; Ashley Jones at Love Not Lost; Barbara Leahy; Bernice Chao, Jessalin Lam, and Suzie Bao at Asians in Advertising; Bronwyn Saglimbeni; Burke Morley; *Campaign*; Carla Fernandez; Caskey Ebeling; Cherie Healey at Siren; Colleen Moffett; Corey Leung; Dave Koranda at University of Oregon; Elizabeth Robillard; Elizabeth Spaulding; Emy diGrappa at What's Your Why?; Erin Dhruva; *Fast Company*; Folayo Lasaki at WIMMIES; The Fran Hauser; Gabrielle Gonzalez at Change.org; Holly Cook; Izzy Chan; Jackie Crynes; Jeff Hilimire at Dragon Army; James Fenton and Vincent Tam of Omnicom; Jen Hedrick; Jen Marples; Jenni Hamilton; Jessica Clifton at Female Forward; Jessica Joines at Womens Purpose Community; Jonas Vail; Kate and Pete Fulford; Kate Webster; Katherine Wintsch of The Mom Complex; Christopher Blair; Keely Ferguson Blair; Kiki Koroshetz at Goop; Laura Keldorf; Leslie Bee and Omniwomen; Libby Holl; Linda Sivertsen at Book Mama; Lindsay Shookus and Kristin O'Keefe Merrick of Women Work Fucking Hard; Lisa Cieslak at GMR; Mark Pollard at Sweathead; Marvin Chow and Laura Young at Google; Margaret Johnson, Meredith Vellines, and Monica Chavez at

GS&P; Melody Chung at Apple; Meredith Latham; Mimi Su; Molly Tuttle; Nancy Koehn at Omnicom University; Nancy Reyes; Nancy Vaughn at White Book Agency; Nancy Vonk and Janet Kestin at Swim; Ophira Edut of Astro Twins; Patrice Poltzer; Peri Higgins, Jaye West, and the team at Evolve Advisors; Raja Sampathi at Calm Corporate; Renee O'Neil; Regan Nelson at *This or Something Better*; Rich Weinstein at VCU Brand Center; Robert Riccardi; Samantha Eddy at Womentum; Sandi Mendelson; Sarah Gormley; Sarah Lent; Scott Shigeoka; Serin Silva at Future Ready CMO; South by Southwest; Stephanie Phillips and Remi Trang; Talya Fisher at Accenture; Tami Kent; Todd Smith; the women of the 2020 Vision Retreat; Theresa Collins at Wieden+Kennedy; the women of The What Alliance; and the women entrepreneurs from the inaugural 3 Percent Accelerator conference.

To our extended family, tribe of friends, and my lifelong girlfriends. You know who you are. Thank you for being my oxygen, fuel, and lifelines. You are the true social security.

Caskey Ebeling, Cyndi Yee, Elle Harrison, Kristyn Carr, Laura Keldorf, Salam Darwaza, Stephanie Lopez, Stephanie Phillips, and Valentine Giraud, you know that I know why we walk this life together.

Reverence and gratitude to the poets, wisdom guides, and wordsmiths who sculpted and shaped me as a spiritual being. While the exercises and tools on these pages are born from strategy, the knowing came from you. David Brooks, David Whyte, Douglas Abrams, Eckhart Tolle, Jack Kornfield, Jane Goodall, Lee Mun Wah, Pema Chödrön, Roger Housden, Stephen Cope, Thich Nhat Hanh.

To the strategy teachers and titans who continue to shape my craft. I stand on your shoulders: Adam Morgan, Adam Stagliano, Andy Grayson, Christine Chen, Diane Tompkins, Graham North, Lorraine Ketch, Jane Gundell, Jon Steel, John Thorpe, Johnny Bauer, Kelly Evans Pfeiffer, Pam Scott. To Adama Sall, Briana Patrick, Etienne Ma, Ginny Ryder, Jane Warren, Mary Gray Johnson, Ralph Paone, Whitney Thomas, thank you for your feedback in vital moments. To the GS&P Strategy Department past, present, and future—there is no better community of strategists and humans . . . in our industry . . . in any industry. I am lucky to be in your constellation.

And finally, to the courageous clients who demand and defend creativity in a world that prefers to play it safe. We need more of you.

BIBLIOGRAPHY

- Anonymous, Aaron. May 2022. Interview with Life Brief participants by Bonnie Wan.

- Anonymous, Barbara. December 2022. Interview with Life Brief participants by Bonnie Wan.

- Anonymous, Beth. December 2022. Interview with Life Brief participants by Bonnie Wan.

- Anonymous, Carmen and Dan. July 2022. Interview with Life Brief participants by Bonnie Wan.

- Anonymous, Diane. September 2021. Interview with Life Brief participants by Bonnie Wan.

- Anonymous, Kelly. 2022. Interview with Life Brief participants by Bonnie Wan.

- Anonymous, Lauren. 2020. Interview with Life Brief participants by Bonnie Wan.

- Anonymous, Reagan. May 2022. Interview with Life Brief participants by Bonnie Wan.

- Anonymous, Samuel. November 2020. Interview with Life Brief participants by Bonnie Wan.

- Anonymous, Sarah. December 2022. Interview with Life Brief participants by Bonnie Wan.

• Anonymous, Susan. January 2023. Interview with Life Brief participants by Bonnie Wan.

• Baldele, Alexander. "The History of Automatic Writing from the Surrealists to AI Writing into the Future." Wendy Network. January 28, 2021. https://wendy.network/the-history-of-automatic-writing-from-the -surrealists-to-ai-writing-into-the-future/.

• Beard, Colin, and John P. Wilson. *Experiential Learning: A Handbook for Education, Training and Coaching.* London: Kogan Page, 2013.

• Brooks, David. *The Second Mountain.* New York: Random House, 2019.

• Burnett, Bill, and Evans, Dave. *Designing Your Life: How to Build a Well-Lived, Joyful Life.* New York: Knopf, 2016.

• Cortizo, Mari Pilar. "Design of a rug" concept developed in collaboration at Project Juice, 2001.

• Cortizo, Mari Pilar. "Identify at least three people" concept developed in collaboration at Project Juice, 2001.

• Cortizo, Mari Pilar. "Peak conditions" idea developed in collaboration with Bonnie Wan at Project Juice, 2001.

• Cortizo, Mari Pilar. Tapestry idea developed in collaboration with Bonnie Wan at Project Juice, 2001.

• Cortizo, Mari Pilar. "What makes me, me? What's my superpower as a strategist?" question developed in collaboration with Bonnie Wan at Project Juice, 2001.

• Engel, Susan. "Many Kids Ask Fewer Questions When They Start School. Here's How We Can Foster Their Curiosity." *Time*, February 23, 2021. https://time.com/5941608/schools-questions-fostering-curiousity/.

- Goodby, Jeff. "Jeff Goodby's 5 Vandalism Rules for Advertising Professionals." AdWeek, October 2, 2018. https://www.adweek.com/agencies /jeff-goodbys-5-vandalism-rules-for-advertising-professionals/.

- Hoffeld, David. "Want to Know What Your Brain Does When It Hears a Question?" *Fast Company*, February 21, 2017. https://www.fastcompany .com/3068341/want-to-know-what-your-brain-does-when-it-hears -a-question.

- Housden, Roger. "Let Your Pen Lead." Writing Workshop, 2017.

- Housden, Roger. "Writing Rearranges the Furniture of Our Minds." Writing Workshop, 2017.

- Johnson, Margaret. May 2023. Interview by Bonnie Wan.

- Katie, Byron. "Wisdom 2.0 Workshop." 2017.

- Lee, Charles. "Dr Christine Runyan – the Examined Life & the Power of Self. " HEARTtalk, October 5, 2021. https://hearttalk.com.my/dr -christine-runyan-the-examined-life-the-power-of-self/.

- Lee, Mun Wah, dir. 1994. *The Color of Fear*. StirFry Seminars.

- Lee, Mun Wah. "Racial Equity Workshop." Online. July 2020.

- The Mask You Live In exercise created by Ashanti Branch, M.Ed., founder and executive director of The Ever Forward Club, 2013. Shared by Pam Scott and Diane Tompkins.

- Morgan, Adam. *Eating the Big Fish: How Challenger Brands Can Compete Against Brand Leaders*. New Jersey: John Wiley & Sons, 1999.

- Murray, Don. *Learning by Teaching: Selected Articles on Writing and Teaching*. Boynton/Cook, 1982.

- Ohno, Taiichi. *Toyota Production System*. Boca Raton, FL: Taylor & Francis Group, 1988.

- Pemberton, Sarah. "The Fastest Path There Is to Ask How You Want Questions." "How You Want" idea inspired by a drawing exercise used by Sarah Pemberton in 2019.

- Phillips, Stephanie. Brain Dump exercise shared via personal correspondence, 2016.

- Pollard, Mark. *Strategy Is Your Words*. New York: Mighty Jungle, 2020.

- Porter, Jennifer. "Why You Should Make Time for Self-Reflection (Even if You Hate Doing It)." *Harvard Business Review*, March 27, 2017. https://hbr.org/2017/03/why-you-should-make-time-for-self-reflection-even-if-you-hate-doing-it.

- Silva, Lauren. "7 Grounding Techniques to Try for Anxiety, according to Experts." *Forbes Health*, September 6, 2022. https://www.forbes.com/health/mind/grounding-techniques-for-anxiety/.

- "Stranger's Eyes" idea developed by Katy Hill, 2022.

- Suttie, Jill. "Why Curious People Have Better Relationships." *Greater Good Magazine*, May 31, 2017. https://greatergood.berkeley.edu/article/item/why_curious_people_have_better_relationships.

- Thomas DeLong's Omnicom University Extension online class, 2021.

- Tuttle, Molly. March 2022. Interview by Bonnie Wan.

- Waldman, Katy. "Joyce Carol Oates Doesn't Prefer Blondes." *The New Yorker*, September 25, 2022. https://www.newyorker.com/culture/the-new-yorker-interview/joyce-carol-oates-doesnt-prefer-blondes.

- Whyte, David. *The Three Marriages*. New York: Riverhead, 2009.

- Whyte, David. *What to Remember When Waking: The Disciplines of Everyday Life*. New Jersey: Sounds True, 2010.

INDEX

A

Aaron, 148–151
abundance, stating one's desire for, 65, 70
action(s). *See also* exercises
importance of small, daily, 164–171
that align with your beliefs, 52–53
activating your Life Brief, 139–140
allowing unexpected events to
happen, 141–145
by being guided by your Life Brief,
147–151
creative courageous living and,
155–161
honoring responsibilities and
housekeeping during, 180–190
how you want to show up and,
181–188
mourning what was and, 191–194
saying yes to serendipity, 145–146
support from others and, 177–179
through focus on small, daily actions,
163–171
your peak conditions and, 173–175
advertising. *See also* brand strategy/
strategists
captivating attention in, 128
goal of tattooing an idea in the minds
of others, 135
"Got Milk?" tagline in, 134–135
tensions in, 56–57
"thought starters" used in, 116
advice, interviewing your fans and, 85
Airbnb, 74
alcohol use/abuse, 27–31

Align Your Beliefs with Your Values
exercise, 52–53
aliveness
creative, courageous living and,
159–161
interviewing your fans about your
peak, 84
peak conditions and, 174–175
anxiety, 6, 22, 67–68, 174
Apple (company), 74
Asians/Asian Americans. *See also* Wan,
Bonnie
in author's life during college, 44
in *The Color of Fear* (documentary),
45–46
invisibility and, 46
assimilation, 37, 44–45, 46, 48–49
authentic selves, 40. *See also* inner voice/
inner self

B

Barbara, 31, 32, 106, 107
behavior, aligning your beliefs with your,
52–53
beliefs. *See also* limiting beliefs
"activating" your, 53
aligning your behavior with your,
52–53
uncovering our, 41–42
belonging, feeling of, 36–38, 48
Ben & Jerry's, 56–57
"Be Rich in Relationship," 134
Beth, 202
Black Lives Matter, 46

INDEX

INDEX

ABOUT THE AUTHOR

Bonnie Wan is an author, speaker, and a partner at the world-renowned advertising agency Goodby Silverstein & Partners. Bonnie has been celebrated as Chief Strategy Officer of the Year, an Adweek 50 honoree, and an AdAge Leading Woman. She was named to AdAge's 2023 Class of Leading Women and as 2022's Chief Strategy Officer of the Year. As the creator of the Life Brief, Bonnie helps people live with greater clarity, creativity, and courage by teaching them how to write briefs for their lives. The Life Brief is a practice based on her belief that "you cannot have it all, but you can have all that matters." The Life Brief has evolved from an agency talk into a workbook, workshops, and speaking appearances at SXSW, Google, Apple, Jane Goodall's Activating Hope Summit, Gwyneth Paltrow's Goop, the 3% Conference, Accenture, Bain & Company, and Change.org. It has now evolved into the book you see before you. Bonnie lives in Northern California with her husband, four kids, and Charlie the dog.